Using Stories for Professional Development

This book offers a selection of stories about teaching, learning, and school life that you can use in a variety of PD formats and settings.

Grouped into four categories—students, teachers, administrators, and parents—these tales offer a powerful entry point for thinking and reflecting on your school environment in a new and meaningful way. Each brief tale is presented to spark a 10–15 minute group discussion that will help educators think more deeply about the complex, human problems they confront on a daily basis. Suggested questions and a brief commentary following each tale can be used to explore the issues embedded in the tale and, thereby, empower staff to generate creative responses to them.

Ditch your "sit and get" professional development and "tap into the wisdom of the ages" by using these powerful tales to give educators the gift of time to think and talk about what it really means to educate hearts and minds.

James Dillon has been an educator for over 40 years and is currently an educational consultant for Measurement Incorporated, which sponsors the Center for Leadership and Bullying Prevention.

Also Available from Routledge Eye On Education
(www.routledge.com/k-12)

Essential Truths for Principals
Danny Steele and Todd Whitaker

**Building Effective Professional Development in Elementary School:
Designing a Path for Excellent Teaching**
Judy Johnson

**Your First Year:
How to Survive and Thrive as a New Teacher**
Todd Whitaker, Katherine Whitaker, Madeline Whitaker Good

Classroom Management from the Ground Up
Todd Whitaker, Katherine Whitaker, Madeline Whitaker Good

**101 Answers for New Teachers and Their Mentors:
Effective Teaching Tips for Daily Classroom Use, 3rd Edition**
Annette Breaux

**Passionate Learners:
How to Engage and Empower Students, 2nd Edition**
Pernille Ripp

**75 Ways to Be a Better Teacher Tomorrow:
With Less Stress and Quick Success**
Annette Breaux and Todd Whitaker

**Professional Development:
What Works, 3rd Edition**
Sally J. Zepeda

**Using Stories for Professional Development:
35 Tales to Promote Reflection and Discussion in Schools**
James Dillon

Using Stories for Professional Development

35 Tales to Promote Reflection and Discussion in Schools

James Dillon

Routledge
Taylor & Francis Group
NEW YORK AND LONDON

First published 2020
by Routledge
52 Vanderbilt Avenue, New York, NY 10017

and by Routledge
2 Park Square, Milton Park, Abingdon, Oxon, OX14 4RN

Routledge is an imprint of the Taylor & Francis Group, an informa business

© 2020 Taylor & Francis

The right of James Dillon to be identified as author of this work has been asserted by him in accordance with sections 77 and 78 of the Copyright, Designs and Patents Act 1988.

All rights reserved. No part of this book may be reprinted or reproduced or utilized in any form or by any electronic, mechanical, or other means, now known or hereafter invented, including photocopying and recording, or in any information storage or retrieval system, without permission in writing from the publishers.

Trademark notice: Product or corporate names may be trademarks or registered trademarks, and are used only for identification and explanation without intent to infringe.

Library of Congress Cataloging-in-Publication Data
A catalog record for this title has been requested

ISBN: 978-0-367-20358-0 (hbk)
ISBN: 978-0-367-20359-7 (pbk)
ISBN: 978-0-429-26108-4 (ebk)

Typeset in Palatino
by Wearset Ltd, Boldon, Tyne and Wear

Contents

Acknowledgments vi
Meet the Author viii

Introduction: Connecting the Dots 1

1   **Why This Book?** 7

2   **How to Use This Book** 17

3   **Student Tales** 25

4   **Teacher Tales** 67

5   **Administrator Tales** 115

6   **Parent Tales** 159

Acknowledgments

I am extremely grateful to Routledge for taking a chance on publishing a book that is so unlike other professional books. It is simply a book of stories designed to provoke thought and discussion among educators. It is a book that I thoroughly enjoyed writing.

I am so fortunate that I found an editor, Lauren Davis, who, based on her experience as a teacher, saw the value and benefits of such a book. Lauren's enthusiastic support for the idea behind this book provided me with the confidence and commitment to dig deep into my professional memory for these stories. Every day that I wrote this book, I would pinch myself to make sure that it wasn't a dream. Thank you, Lauren, for making this dream come true for me.

I wish to thank my colleagues and friends at Measurement Incorporated and the New York State Center for School Safety where I work part time. I would especially like to thank Tom Kelsh, my friend, colleague and vice president of Measurement Incorporated (MI). His unwavering support for my work has enabled me to continue to grow as an educator and to share my experience with other educators.

I am grateful to other colleagues at the New York State Center for School Safety: Tina Tierney, Kathy O'Boyski-Butler, and Willie Freeman. We are a great team. Our shared visits and interactions with schools in New York State have provided me with new stories of heroic educators working in difficult situations. Our shared observations and discussions have helped to deepen my understanding of the challenges that are still facing our schools today.

I would especially like to thank two other colleagues and friends, Casey Bardin and Diana Straut. They have listened to many of my stories and shared their own stories with me. I have adapted and customized a few of these stories in this book. They are creative, reflective, and caring educators, and people whom I feel grateful to know.

Two other long-time colleagues and friends, Nancy Andress and Corrine Falope, continue to provide great encouragement and support for my writing. Our conversations and shared vision of education continues to guide my work.

My four grown children, Ernie, Tim, Brian and Hannah have busy and productive lives of their own. They continue to give me the time and support to listen to my stories and my ideas. Seeing them grow from children into loving and caring adults has been the greatest story of my life.

As I wrote this book, I was truly blessed to see my two twin grandsons, Conrad and Tucker, learn and grow in front of my eyes. Observing the wonder of human development from a grandparent's perspective, unburdened of the responsibilities of parenthood, has given me great joy, appreciation and insight into how loving and trusting relationships are the foundation for all learning.

Finally, nothing I do or achieve is possible without the constant love and support of my wife, Louisa. Her career as a school social worker, and now as a volunteer in charitable work in her retirement, is really the best story I can imagine for showing what it means to be a loving and caring person who is continually making the world a better place. For Louisa, this is a never-ending story.

Meet the Author

James Dillon has been an educator for over 40 years, including 20 years as a school administrator.

While principal of Lynnwood Elementary in New York, he developed the Peaceful School Bus Program, designed to prevent and reduce bullying. He subsequently wrote *The Peaceful School Bus* (Hazelden, 2008) a facilitator's guide for implementing the program, which is now used in almost every state.

Jim was named Principal of the Year in 2007 by the Greater Capital Region Principal Center. He has also received recognition for administrative leadership for character education.

He is the author of *No Place for Bullying: Leadership for Schools That Care for Every Student* (Corwin, 2012) and *Reframing Bullying Prevention to Build Stronger School Communities* (Corwin 2015), a children's picture book *Okay Kevin* (Jessica Kingsley Publishers, 2017), and a novel for middle readers *Marching with Dr. King* (Create Space, 2017).

He is a regular contributor to Smart Briefs education blog and has had articles published in *Principal Magazine*, *Education Week* and other professional publications. He was also a presenter at TEDx Schenectady 2016.

Jim is currently an educational consultant for Measurement Incorporated, who sponsor the Center for Leadership and Bullying Prevention. He makes presentations and conducts workshops on a variety of educational topics, including instruction, classroom management, leadership, and supervision. Jim has presented at many local, state, and national conferences.

He has four grown children, Ernie, Tim, Brian and Hannah, and two grandchildren. He and his wife, Louisa, a retired school social worker, live in Niskayuna, NY. He can be reached at jdillon117@yahoo.com.

Introduction
Connecting the Dots

After 60 years as a student, teacher, administrator, and consultant, plus my years as a parent guiding four children through school, I have probably seen or heard almost everything that could happen in a school.

With this much experience behind me, I am in a good position to follow the advice that Steve Jobs gave in his commencement address at Stanford University in 2005:

> "You can't connect the dots looking forward; you can only connect them looking backwards. So you have to trust that the dots will somehow connect in your future. Because believing that the dots will connect down the road will give you the confidence to follow your heart even when it leads you off the well worn path; and that will make all the difference."

This book is a product of my effort to make sense of my life in school: an attempt to connect the many dots that have marked my diverse journey. It is a translation of my experience into stories that I hope will resonant with other educators, helping them to reflect and gain insight into their own journey.

Here are the "dots" that I connected to write this book:

Dot #1: Some questions have no answers and some problems cannot be readily solved
Open up any professional book about education and you will find solutions to problems and answers to questions facing schools today. This fact shouldn't be a surprise since two of the main activities of school have always been answering questions and solving problems. Educators, therefore, being goal oriented and outcome focused are always searching for a book that offers answers to questions and solutions for problems.

But can a book realistically address the myriad human issues manifested every day in a school? Not really. Most educators would readily admit that their *real* work involves facing questions that have no immediate answers and problems that resist all attempts to solve them. Instead, educators typically find ambiguity when looking for clarity, complexity when yearning for simplicity, confusion when seeking certainty and frustration when needing solutions.

Regardless of the high degree of difficulty inherent in their job, educators are under immense pressure to perform to certain standards in order to get their students to perform to certain standards. As a result, when they struggle with issues involving their own hearts and minds and those of their students, they think that their job "should" be easier and that they "should" be more competent.

When I look back on my own career and my conversations with other educators, it is now clear to me that struggle is an inherent and constant aspect of interacting with students and colleagues. And wishing that struggle to go away *only gets in the way* of embracing and affirming the important work that educators must do.

Hence, I hesitated for several years before writing another professional book (after writing three of them) because I no longer wanted to contribute to the mistaken notion that educators' struggles could be lessened, if only they absorbed the content of my book, or any book, and applied it to their practice.

Moreover, I am convinced that our constant search for answers and solutions only intensifies the struggle and increases the difficulty of our job. Seeking the program or strategy that will improve our school's climate, get behavioral problems under control and raise test scores, only distracts us from confronting our problems and, consequently, what they have to teach us. To make matters worse, when any solution fails to deliver its promise, our disillusionment grows along with the belief that any change is possible.

Dot #2: My accidental discovery of the power of stories
As an educator who also struggled, I have felt the call to help my colleagues meet their demanding professional and personal challenges.

So, when I retired, it was from a job with a lot of responsibilities, but not from being an educator. I wanted to empower educators: the people at the point of contact with students. I decided to devote my extra time and energy to reading, researching, writing and presenting, so I could help my colleagues in the trenches of the daily grind of working in a school.

As I ventured into the world of professional development using my books as a platform for presenting, I soon began to question how much I was helping by sharing ideas, no matter how interesting or meaningful they might be. Despite my growing doubts, I plugged away making presentations, with slides filled with brief video clips and graphics designed to highlight and enhance those ideas. To warm up my audience and maybe get a few laughs, I started to tell stories from my life and career.

At the one of these workshops I told a story about the tomatoes I grew compared to the ones my brother-in-law grew. Our tomato plants were bought from the same greenhouse. The main point of the story was about how I as a skilled and experienced gardener produced inferior tomatoes to the ones my first-time gardener brother-in-law grew.

He threw the plants into the ground and occasionally watered them, while I painstakingly followed every gardening tip and recommendation I could find. I shared how perplexed and frustrated I was about the differences in our tomatoes until I realized that the difference was in the soil. The soil in my plot was depleted from years of gardening while his plot had fresh, fertile soil. I told this story to emphasize how a school's culture, like soil, would explain why programs or initiatives work in some schools and not others.

Two years later I made a different presentation to basically the same group of people. During the registration period, many people came up to me and asked me about how my tomatoes were doing. I looked at them quizzically until I remembered that I had told them the story about my tomatoes. That made perfect sense—it was an interesting story about something everyone could relate to and *it stuck with them* when I am sure everything on my slides had long since faded from their memory. I realized that giving them something to think about was much more important than delivering the content of my presentation.

Stories have a lot more power than even the best PowerPoint® slide. In this case, an old dog (me) had learned a new trick (that wasn't really new)—the power of stories.

Dot #3: Stories reflect the wisdom of the ages for changing hearts and minds

Prompted by my story about a story, I started to read how businesses were embracing storytelling and the use of narratives in professional development and marketing. At the same time, I read books about spirituality and how people throughout the ages addressed basic questions about life and what it meant to be human: the same questions and intractable problems that educators struggle with today.

Throughout history and cultures, these complexities of life are not addressed through facts, reasoning, and long explanations but rather through the arts: music, painting, sculpture, and storytelling that occur in a communal setting. These traditions developed throughout the ages were based on the idea that people change and grow when their *hearts and minds* are engaged—not just their minds.

The wisdom of the ages confirms the saying that "life is not a problem to be solved but a mystery to be lived." Stories have been a way for us to encounter the mystery of our lives that are filled with the human emotions that flow from our successes and our failures. Stories are designed to help us discover what is in our hearts and minds and then to share what we find with others.

In schools today, however, listening to stories, reflecting on them and discussing them are at best a warm-up act and accessory to what really matters: evidence-based programs implemented with fidelity to achieve measurable goals and outcomes.

Dot #4: The persistence of "mindlessness" in schools

In my visits to schools as a consultant and observer, I have seen caring and competent educators teaching good lessons in every type of educational environment. Yet apart from the particulars of these schools, they all have one consistent characteristic: the rapid pace and movement that everyone adheres to on a daily basis. Perhaps because I was no longer habituated to it, the pace and the efficiencies of the school environment startled me. I felt like calling "time out" so everyone could take a deep breath and connect with each other.

Not surprisingly, I also noticed how infrequently the words, "think and reflect" were uttered in any classroom. Typically, when one lesson was over everyone rushed to the next one. (Not unlike people popping up from their seats and rushing to the exits when the credits start at the end of a movie.)

When I thought about the possible consequences of having no time or space to think, reflect and share in schools, I harkened back to a book I read in 1972 in my first educational foundation course in college: *Crisis in the Classroom*[1] by Charles Silberman.

Charles Silberman was not an educator but a journalist with a background in economics. He had previously written books about race relations and the criminal justice system. He was commissioned by the Carnegie Foundation to observe and report on the American educational system.

With his fresh set of eyes, his most salient observation and critique of schools was the consistent pattern of what he referred to as *mindlessness*, which he described as the failure of educators "to ask why they are doing what they are doing – to think seriously or deeply about the purposes or consequences of education" (p. 11).

Re-reading part of this book almost 50 years later brought to mind this saying: "The more things change the more they remain the same."

This *mindlessness* present in 1970 is still a constant in our schools, and it is a key reason why schools have been immune to meaningful changes over the years.

Having no time or space to think, reflect and share is the best formula for producing and sustaining *mindlessness*.

Connecting the Dots = 35 Tales

So, when I reflected on the power of stories, I realized that they offered a way to put this mindlessness and the constant searching for quick answers and solutions *on hold*. Stories can help us embrace the challenge and the struggle inherent in educating students; they can be a vehicle for gaining greater insight into our own hearts and minds, as well as those of our students.

In addition, I reasoned that listening to tales (*educationally customized stories*) and discussing them in a communal setting could be a modest, yet enjoyable, entry point for interjecting some thinking and reflecting into the school environment.

Listening to and discussing these stories or tales could be a springboard for doing what Silberman recommended almost 50 years ago: "If mindlessness is the central problem, the solution must lie in infusing the various institutions with purpose, more important, with thought about purpose, and about the ways in which techniques, content, and organization fulfill or alter purpose" (p. 11).

So, I looked around for stories that could serve as parables or fables for educators and couldn't find any. Therefore, I decided to use my personal and professional database of over 60 years' experience (as student, parent and educator) to create my own set of school tales … and write this book.

I acknowledge that this book is, to quote Steve Jobs, "off the well worn path" of most professional books and approaches to professional development. I hope, however, that this book offers an alternate *path* to meeting the needs of educators and their students; that it is a positive addition to the other valuable and current initiatives being offered in education.

Ultimately, if it gives a few school leaders the idea (and permission) to carve out a tiny slice of time and space for the hearts and minds of educators to connect through stories, this book will serve a valuable purpose and meet a forgotten need.

To sum it all up: give educators the time and space to listen, think and share … and good things will inevitably follow.

Note

1   Silberman, Charles E. (1970). *Crisis in the classroom: The remaking of American education*. New York, NY: Random House.

1

Why This Book?

There is a simple answer to the question of "why this book"? Because, it's a book educators don't **have to** read. They can listen to it.

Although reading is at the heart of all learning, most educators would probably admit that finding time to read is a luxury few of them can afford.

Educators have a multitude of demands and responsibilities placed on them. They work long hours beyond their time in the classroom. Consequently, it's not surprising that their time for reading boils down to a few minutes before they fall asleep at night. (Ironically, professional books are good sleep inducers—I know, I have written three of them.)

To better understand why educators don't have to read this book, here is a list of **what it does not contain**:

- No program or initiative that promises to solve a problem at school.
- No theory to comprehend or defend.
- No criticism of policies or practices.
- No data to share.
- No data to justify what to do or not do.
- No proposal for increasing student engagement, participation and achievement.
- No research to apply to educational practices.
- No strategy to improve your climate, increase test scores, engage the community or inspire teachers.

- No stated outcomes or goals listed at the start of each chapter.
- No lengthy quotations, no charts or figures, no footnotes or bibliography and only one citation.

Here is **what is in this book**: stories to hear, think about and discuss with colleagues.

Professional Development from Outside In to the Inside Out

Most professional books are concerned with increasing an educator's professional knowledge, so they contain most of what is on that list. These books provide content (*something outside of the educators*) that educators are expected to absorb and ultimately integrate into their practice. The type of professional development reflected in these books offers an *outside in* approach, i.e. adding to or supplying something that is missing from an educator's knowledge base or skill repertoire.

Using Stories for Professional Development: 35 Tales to Promote Reflection and Discussion in Schools deliberately chooses not to have those items from that list. Instead, the book removes this content along with the implication that professionals need to absorb *something more* to get better at their jobs.

For Seinfeld fans, this book could be considered to be about *nothing*: having no "educational content." But the benefit of being about *nothing* removes the distraction of *content to consider*, thereby, allowing educators to look inward to discover and explore their values, beliefs and assumptions and then to share them with colleagues.

Instead of bringing something *outside* to the educators and their school environment to improve it, this approach is *inside out:* bringing what's *inside* educators' hearts and minds *out to* the light of a professional community to foster its growth.

Necessity of Reflection

This inside out process of professional development requires time and space for reflection.

Without reflection, our experiences tend to replicate themselves, only perpetuating established habits of thinking, talking and acting. Meaningful change, therefore, is dependent upon being able to gain perspective: seeing ourselves in the context of our environment. This is extremely difficult for educators, or anyone, to do.

Which is why the saying that "fish would be the last to discover water" rings true: people are sealed into their subjective experience of the world.

John Dewey recognized this difficulty when he said, "We do not learn from experience … we learn from reflecting on experience."

Meaningful reflection, therefore, requires more than just looking at the surface of things; it should provide insight and deepen our thinking. It should help us discover and understand the values and beliefs that underlie our words and actions.

Mental and emotional reflection, like a physical reflection, requires some type of mirror: a way to look outward at ourselves in order to see into ourselves.

All mirrors, however, must be used cautiously. Most people when they unexpectedly see themselves in a mirror are usually taken aback and quickly look away.

For mirrors to be helpful, therefore, they must be gentle and offer a safe way of looking at and seeing who we are.

Seeing Our Scripts

What do we see when we look at ourselves? We see ourselves living out our stories—the ones we write for ourselves.

(This is my way of understanding how we function in the world, formulated from my readings in psychology, sociology, philosophy and my own experiences.)

Beyond the present moment, our lives are essentially stories. What happened yesterday (or even a minute ago) is a re-construction and interpretation of events filtered through our pre-existing values shaped by prior experiences. What will happen in the future is only a projection and prediction based on experiences that have already happened.

This filtering process occurs because it is not possible for us to completely and accurately absorb all of our experiences; there is always too much going on. We need a filter to manage and make sense out of experience. We are, therefore, continually constructing a narrative about what life is and who we are. We write our story and then live it.

This story, or narrative, we create in our minds serves as an *internal script* that guides what we do and say in response to our experiences. These scripts help us maintain a sense of consistency, order and predictability.

These scripts, however, are works-in-progress, always *subject to change*. It's similar to testing a theory or hypothesis to see if it matches the facts. We try out our scripts by interacting with others who have their own scripts.

Learning and growing, therefore, is a process of incorporating new and different experiences into our current script and then expanding and adapting it.

While our scripts are necessary navigation tools, they also can impede our learning for the following reasons:

- ♦ A script is like a pair of glasses. When we look at the world with glasses, we don't see our glasses. Similarly, when we perceive the world we don't see our script, so we think we see an unfiltered, objective reality and not our version of it, shaped by our script.
- ♦ Our scripts cannot account for the range of experiences we have. We tend to either ignore or resist new information that contradicts our existing script.
- ♦ Adjusting and adapting our script to account for the new and different information often creates discomfort, uncertainty and confusion.
- ♦ How much we learn therefore depends upon how we manage this stress of discovering that our script doesn't account for new and different experiences.

As a result of these problems, we can easily deceive ourselves: we think we know what is really happening when we have a limited understanding of it. This is why we stick to our scripts and think that no other version of reality is possible.

Flipping Our Scripts

Becoming unstuck from our script usually requires a disruptive event or a series of troubling experiences: a death, an illness, a betrayal, a divorce, or any type of failure. These events signal to us that our script needs adjustment; what has gone before cannot account for what just happened. These unexpected and unwanted experiences can subtly or radically change how we view the world and ourselves: our scripts are flipped.

When our script is flipped, we simultaneously discover: that we had a script, what that script was and how incomplete it was. This discovery can be disorienting and stressful, however necessary it might be.

Ask most people about an experience when they learned the most and they will describe a crisis, problem, and/or disruption in their lives—**not** a time when everything was going as planned. They were stopped in their tracks and couldn't function as they had in the past—not a good feeling to have. As a result, most of us do not want, nor like, having our scripts flipped.

The irony, however, is that having our script flipped is a much better and healthier alternative than staying stuck in a script. Having our script flipped is an opportunity, albeit in disguise, for learning and growth.

We are caught in this paradox: the experiences that flip our script are a deep source of learning and growth; they are exactly those experiences we desperately seek to avoid.

To learn from these experiences, therefore, we need **a safer way** to see ourselves, without the disorientation and distress of directly experiencing our scripts being flipped.

Stories: Safe and Gentle Mirrors

Throughout the ages, stories have been the safer way for dealing with this paradox: that we learn the most from the experiences we most want to avoid.

Stories are a gentle mirror. When we vicariously identify with a character whose script is played out and flipped in front of us, we can get a clearer vision of our own script.

Stories allow us to compare and contrast the characters' scripts with our own. When we see how characters react to having their scripts flipped, we can reflect on what we would do in a similar situation. We gain insight into the problems precipitated by the script that the character was following. Stories help us step safely out of our own scripts to see the possibilities that our scripts might have blinded us from seeing.

Stories prepare us. Stories can warn us of what is to come. Stories can re-assure us.

When the characters in a story survive and grow stronger from confronting their challenges, we can envision ourselves doing the same.

Stories show a way out, a choice, an "out of the box" idea that we might not have imagined until we looked through the eyes of the character in the story.

Most importantly, stories offer hope in moments of doubt and struggle—they can keep us going when it seems like we are stuck and getting nowhere fast.

Problems of the Heart

Although some problems at school have workable solutions, the most important ones involve people living and learning together: the ones dealing with concerns of the human heart. These problems are not so much solved, as much as they must be embraced and lived. This aspect of life in school is often forgotten or ignored in our professional discourse.

As a result, educators rarely get the support they need to confront these complex problems of the heart and mind. Too often, they are told that they must find the answers and solutions in programs, research and data.

But most educators know in their hearts that they need something different, something that will sustain their spirit as they grapple with the challenges of living and learning in school.

Using Stories for Professional Development: 35 Tales to Promote Reflection and Discussion in Schools tries to meet that need that educators often have difficulty articulating.

This book relies on stories, i.e., people's scripts interacting with each other, to help educators gain greater insight into the emotional and psychological dimensions of the challenges they face in school, the same challenges that have confronted human beings throughout the ages.

Yet, as much as stories and reflecting on them have been used throughout the ages as a source of learning, this tradition has not been typically a part of professional development.

Barriers to Meaningful Reflection

Although meaningful reflection should be at the center of professional growth, providing that opportunity in schools today is very problematic.

Here is a summary of the types of logistical, structural, and psychological barriers that hold educators back from this type of reflection and discussion:

Little time: This time-crunch is endemic to all schools. Limited time plus increased demands and diminished resources can hinder the growth of even the most motivated educator: *when you are trying to keep your head above water, it's hard to think about swimming to the shore.*

Activity bias: School leaders, pressured to improve their schools, often feel compelled to propose changes to their staff (even if there is no indication that the proposed change will make things "better"), because doing something often feels "better" than doing nothing. When proposals/action plans fail to produce positive change, many veteran staff members typically ignore or resist new initiatives knowing that "these too shall pass."

Structural inertia: Many educational practices, because they are embedded in what we know as school, are invisible *givens* that resist change: *institutionalized scripts*. Any suggestion of changing them can trigger understandable discomfort among educators. Not only does this structural level of change seem impossible, the amount of work and planning required to make these changes are a deterrent even for those who might agree with those changes.

Tip of the iceberg conversations: Many professional conversations get sabotaged because the participants don't realize that their opinions reflect deeply held assumptions, embedded in their scripts. As a result, many conflicts in professional conversations appear intractable because each person's "reality" bears little resemblance to anyone else's.

Pressure of outcomes: There seems to be an unwritten rule that anything presented to educators must be preceded by a statement of outcomes that are expected as a result of that presentation. Educators are constantly told that every interaction must be planned and managed toward some pre-conceived end. This rule leaves little time for "creative meanderings" i.e., freer and deeper explorations of what is possible in schools.

Purpose and Function of the 35 Tales

Listening to, reflecting on and talking about stories can serve as a "work around" for these barriers that inhibit and stall many professional conversations.

Using Stories for Professional Development: 35 Tales to Promote Reflection and Discussion in Schools attempts to do so by offering brief tales* about teaching, learning and life in school.

(*Tales convey a straightforward description of events whereas a short story usually involves a more detailed narrative involving characters and other literary devices.)

The tales can serve as a vehicle for discovering and revealing perspectives, values and beliefs of the participants who hear and discuss them.

Each tale entertains and intrigues by offering familiar scenarios with a twist. The tales will blend the expected with the unexpected: they will flip the scripts of their characters.

This book hopes (in a good way) to smuggle "meaningful reflection" past this invisible but resistant barrier that exists in most schools. These tales will be designed to stimulate thinking and discussion with "no strings attached": educators should not be expected to do anything different as a result of listening, thinking and talking.

These tales were developed and shaped from real life experiences in schools from the point of view of students, teachers, school leaders and parents. They are meant to be a gift, a break from the norm, and a way to allow educators to sit and listen with colleagues, as if they were sitting around a campfire hearing stories.

A small amount of time, less than 15 minutes once a month, set aside for educators to hear stories and discuss them, can provide mutual support and understanding for confronting the questions that have no easy answers and the problems that resist solutions.

Using Stories for Professional Development: 35 Tales to Promote Reflection and Discussion in Schools is based on the belief that positive change and creative responses to challenges are more likely to occur in schools where educators have explored and shared their values, beliefs and assumptions about teaching and learning. This is the foundation for members of the school community to decide how to re-write their own script and collectively re-write the script for their school.

This book, when used appropriately in professional gatherings, can affirm the identity of educators as reflective thinkers, empowered colleagues and creative agents of change for their school communities.

Fundamentally, the value of *Using Stories for Professional Development: 35 Tales to Promote Reflection and Discussion in Schools* comes from its belief that if educators are given the space and time to listen, reflect and talk with each other, they will collectively discover what they need to do to improve their practice, their school and *be willing to do it.*

Summary

Using Stories for Professional Development: 35 Tales to Promote Reflection and Discussion in Schools does the following:

- Holds a gentle mirror up for educators to reflect on their daily experiences in school.
- Helps educators gain insight into their own values, beliefs and assumptions about teaching and learning, through their vicarious reaction to the unpredictable twists that characters experience in the stories,
- Helps educators realize that how they function in the school is a by-product of their script and not a fixed reality that they are obliged to follow.
- Nudges educators in a safe, supportive environment to explore opportunities for how they can *flip their scripts* and re-write them: change how they think about school and consequentially change how they act in school.

Using Stories for Professional Development: 35 Tales to Promote Reflection and Discussion in Schools flips the script of traditional professional development from an *outside in* process to an *inside out* one by helping educators realize that they already have, within and among themselves, all the resources they need to create and sustain the type of school they want and that their students need and deserve.

2

How to Use This Book

Using Stories for Professional Development: 35 Tales to Promote Reflection and Discussion in Schools is designed to be a tool for professional development with no pre-determined outcomes. The book is based on the simple premise that individual and collective professional growth will occur if educators are given more time to think and talk with each other. Like any tool, however, the people who hold it in their hands will determine how it is used and how well it is used.

Here are some questions to consider before using the tales in the book:

Who Could Use the Book?

A principal who wants to promote reflective thinking and professional discussion could use this book in a faculty meeting, during professional development days, or with any small group of staff.

Faculty at a school of education might use the book with a class of prospective educators.

Mentors could use this book with those they are supporting/coaching.

A self-directed group of educators might use the book to explore their values and beliefs about teaching and learning.

Who Should Decide to Use the Book?

To avoid having another idea shot down or sabotaged by some staff, it would be preferable to share the idea for using this book with some type of shared decision-making team in the school. If such a team does not exist, a school leader could gather an informal group of staff to discuss the idea and enlist their feedback and hopefully their support in using it.

A school leader could ask for volunteers to try out the book in a small group setting. That group could offer input on to how to use the book in the future. The more the idea for using this book emanates from staff, rather than just the school leader, the greater the chance it will be welcomed by the rest of the staff.

How to Introduce the Idea of Using These Tales for Professional Development?

Enthusiastic school leaders should avoid announcing that there is a new professional development activity they are excited about using with their (unsuspecting) staff.

Just as a new program or initiative is met with skepticism and/or resistance, reading a simple tale and discussing it might not be a welcome activity for some. What might otherwise seem like a simple request could be perceived as a waste of time. If staff members don't understand the purpose and value of listening to a story, then even the most intriguing story could be met with deaf ears.

Every school leader should understand that using this book is a deviation from the norm of most professional development activities. They would be wise to heed this advice from one veteran administrator I knew: always put anything new into a familiar package.

Packaging is another term for "framing." How something is framed, to a large extent, determines how it is perceived. Positive framing works better than negative framing. For example, people respond better to the message of "eating healthy to live better" as opposed to the message that they must "diet to lose weight."

The use of this book should be framed as a positive change from the typical "here's the new idea that will improve the status quo" type of professional development. The process of listening to and talking about stories should be framed as an affirmation of a staff's collective experience and wisdom.

When to Use These 35 Tales?

Rather than creating a new time for staff to listen to a tale and discuss it, it would be preferable to fit it into an existing meeting that has been established and accepted as part of the school's schedule. Most schools typically have monthly staff meetings for approximately one hour. Other schools have grade level meetings, curriculum meetings, or a variety of planning meetings.

If possible, it would be beneficial to have the entire staff listening and responding to a tale at the same time. This would create a common experience and subsequent memory among the staff. A tale that resonates with a staff could become a valuable reference point for future discussions that have more definite outcomes attached to them.

When the reading of a tale and its subsequent discussion can be fitted into an established meeting, it will more likely be viewed as a positive respite from the topics and tasks that make up typical faculty/staff meetings.

The tales are less than 1,000 words and can be read aloud in about 5–7 minutes, with a similar amount of time devoted to discussing them, so that the activity should last no more than 15 minutes. Ultimately, each staff should determine for themselves the best time for listening to and discussing these tales.

How to Select the Tales to be Read?

The four categories (student, teacher, administrator, parent) can be viewed as a menu of perspectives on school.

Staff can select a tale that is pertinent to their interests or current concerns.

The tales are not in any sequence, although some of them do form contrasting pairs. In one tale there might be a teacher who is more open, while in another tale a teacher might be more rigid. Similarly, one tale could be about a diligent student, while another tale is about a student who is frequently in trouble. These tales could be read and listened to over consecutive sessions.

How to Present the Tales?

Ideally each tale should be read aloud, either to the whole group or in each small group. Although it might seem like a minor detail, there is a benefit to having each person hear the tale instead of having individuals read it silently.

Hearing the tale read aloud creates a shared experience. Staff members could read along with a copy of the tale in front of them, but they would still be hearing the tale in the same way as their colleagues.

In addition, since the tales depict interactions among characters, reading them aloud can create more vivid images in people's minds that are more likely to stick in their memories.

Having staff members who are skilled at reading stories aloud, or who have some acting background, would enhance the experience of listening to them. There is also the option of giving staff copies of the tale to read prior to the meeting, but it is recommended that the tale still be read aloud at the meeting.

What Arrangements are Needed?

Ideally staff should be sitting in small groups so that they can easily see and hear each member of the group. Staff could sit at tables or in chair circles. Cooperative learning practice typically recommends having groups of no more than four, to ensure that every participant gets to contribute to the discussion. This might not be feasible for many reasons, but each group should not exceed eight people. The higher the number of participants, the less time there would be for each to contribute to the discussion.

How Should the Listening/Discussion be Structured?

This is a very important aspect of the activity to consider. Each small group should have a facilitator for each session (staff can take turns assuming this role). This facilitator could also be the person designated to read the tale aloud for the small group, if reading aloud to the large group is not preferred. There should be a designated timekeeper to give a one-minute warning when the discussion time is about to end.

Careful consideration should be given to the time after the tale is read so that each participant can reflect and react to the story before hearing the thoughts of other participants.

Participants should have a private, quiet time to contemplate their response. This time period could be about 30 seconds. Staff could jot down their responses to the tale or, if they choose to, just sit and think.

Following this quiet time for reflection, there are two recommended ways of proceeding:

- ♦ Have individuals turn to a partner and briefly share their response to the story. Again, the time period could be 30 seconds per person for a total of one minute.
- ♦ Proceed in round robin fashion with each person sharing their response without others making any comments.

After each person has had time to think and share, the facilitator can open up the discussion to the small group. The facilitator's main responsibility is to make sure that all voices are heard in the subsequent discussion and prevent one loud or emotional voice from dominating the discussion.

What Should Happen Following Small Group Discussion?

Depending upon the time available, the facilitator of the meeting could provide a brief time for people to offer comments to the whole group.

Should there be Any Ground Rules for the Discussion?

Each group could decide this for themselves. Some groups might need a stated rule of "no interrupting another person" but other groups might have already established this as a social norm. Some groups could borrow ground rules from other trainings or just transfer ground rules that have worked for other groups or committees. To simplify things, groups could start without ground rules at first and then decide to establish them later on as the need arises.

What Should Happen Following the End of the Time Allotted to this Activity?

Nothing. Avoid the urge to ask: So, what now? The best response following the session would be for the participants to thank each other and move on to the next part of the scheduled meeting. If people are stimulated by the tale and want to keep talking they can do so on their own time. Remember this activity carries a "no strings attached" label.

Other Considerations

Questions
The questions provided at the end of each tale are optional. Each group could decide to discuss the tale without using the questions. The group however might find that one or two questions are needed to jump start the discussion. Each group can determine the protocol for answering questions. Each person in the group can have a turn to respond to a question. A question could also be posed to the group and anyone could respond. The questions could also be provided to each member of the group to assist them during their private reflection time.

Comments

The comments were not written to be part of the group discussion. They might be used for those group members who feel the need to further explore the issues raised in the tale and the subsequent discussion. The comments do not, however, provide an answer to any of the questions nor should they be viewed as evidence to support any member's response. Participants could read the comments on their own time.

Debates

A tale might provoke a strong emotional response for members of the group. As a result, there is the possibility that some members might engage in a debate about the tale and the issues raised by it. Although the best discussions emerge when there are conflicting views, given the limited time for discussion, members of the group might just agree to disagree and find a later time when they could talk at length. Remember, the tales were written to raise questions that have no right answers.

Listening

All staff members should share the goal of becoming better listeners. It is typically easier for educators to talk than to listen. Discussions, however, are more meaningful when people listen to affirm one another's statements before disagreeing with them. These tales could be viewed as practice sessions for listening because there are no strings attached to them: nothing is proposed that might affect what staff are asked to do in the future. As staff members improve their listening skills in response to these tales, other discussions with more concrete implications should become more productive.

Relationships

These tales are designed to explore values and beliefs that often remain hidden to individuals and their peers. For instance, it is possible that someone might not have thought about an assumption he/she holds. In addition, colleagues might work together for years without knowing each other's values and beliefs about teaching and learning. As the tales and subsequent discussions reveal the values, beliefs or assumptions of colleagues, some might be alarmed to discover these differences. Although initially many might prefer not to know about differences with colleagues, over time, discovering them and becoming comfortable with talking about them will strengthen relationships and increase trust among staff members.

Tales Create More Tales

Every educator has a treasure trove of experiences that can be translated into great tales that others would benefit from hearing. Hopefully the experience of listening to these tales and talking about them will help staff members remember and value their own stories. These staff generated tales can be substituted for those in this book.

Have Some Fun

Listening to and talking about these tales should be an enjoyable experience, similar to going to a good movie and talking about it with a spouse or friend. Carving out a time in a busy school day for doing so should not be viewed as a frivolous exercise, but rather as a sign of respect for the collective wisdom of the school staff.

Giving staff the opportunity to play around with ideas can plant the seeds for creative responses to the problems that naturally arise in school. Hopefully, staff members will embrace their collective agency for making their school a better place for everyone and have fun doing so.

Happy listening, thinking and sharing!

3

Student Tales

1

Lost Imagination

Nobody worked harder than Sarah, especially with schoolwork. Her parents never had to tell her to do her homework. She went right to her desk as soon as she got home each day and finished it well before dinner. Sometimes her parents had to tell her to watch a little TV just to relax a bit.

Of course, to her teachers Sarah was a dream come true. She was the one held up as a positive example to her peers. When she finished her own work, she was always ready to help any student who needed it.

Already in fourth grade, Sarah envisioned herself in high school, college and getting a Ph.D., so she could be a professor who taught students and continued to learn.

Sarah particularly loved to read and do research. She would go to the library on the weekend and take out books on her favorite topics: insects, extinct animals, the civil rights movement, and famous women in history.

Her teacher, however, encouraged her to read stories, but she only read historical fiction. She didn't care much for fantasy, science fiction or books about relationships. She didn't see much point in made up stories. There was so much to learn about the world—why should she waste time reading about things that weren't true?

Her teacher distributed folders every morning that contained the assignments that students had to complete that day. Sarah was always eager to check them over to see what she would be learning. The assignment sheets were on the left side of the folder. When Sarah completed one sheet, she moved it to the right side. At the end of the day, she loved the feeling of seeing the left side empty and the right side full.

One day, however, in the middle of the assignment sheets, she spotted a blank sheet except for these words on top: 'Write a totally make-believe story—let your imagination go—have fun!' She had written stories before but none that had to be make-believe. She started trying to think of a story, but each time it was about something that she had done before. She immediately knew it would be boring. What if she couldn't move the sheet from the left side to the right side of the folder? Now her anxiety turned into a panic. What if she didn't have an imagination or she had lost it?

Her teacher noticed a look on Sarah's face that she had never seen before. She walked over and squatted next to her and asked, "Sarah, what's wrong?" Sarah pointed to the blank sheet asking her to use her imagination and replied, "I don't think I can do this assignment. Maybe I don't have an imagination."

Her teacher didn't try to answer that question, but said,

> You know this is a beautiful spring day, and I think our class needs to get some fresh air. We are going outside; why don't you walk around by yourself for a while and see what happens? We can worry about the assignment later.

The school was next to a wooded area so Sarah, who liked animals and plants, decided to walk along the edge of it. She noticed a rabbit hopping down a trail into a hole and a chipmunk scooting up an oak tree. She glanced into the sky and saw three robins disappear into the leaves at the top of the tree. She looked at some dead branches on the ground and saw a caterpillar crawling on one. She spotted a ladybug sitting on a leaf of a wildflower.

Sarah walked over to a big smooth rock next to a tree and sat on it. Then she closed her eyes and leaned back on the tree. Next thing she heard was her teacher ringing a bell to call the class in.

Once inside her teacher said, "Boys and girls, wasn't it great to be outside? I will let you pick any assignment sheet and work on it for a while."

Sarah went right to the blank sheet that had frightened her. She picked up her pencil and started to write non-stop until she heard her teacher say it was lunchtime. Sarah looked at the clock and was surprised that 20 minutes had gone by, like it had just disappeared. Her teacher saw her smiling and went over to her.

"Sarah how did you make out? I see you did the imagination assignment. Can I read it?" Sarah handed it to her teacher, who silently read it:

> Once upon a time there was a girl who thought she lost her imagination, so she went into the woods to look for it. She looked under a rock to see if it was there but it wasn't. She saw a bunny hop into a hole and wondered if he took it. Then she saw three robins fly to the top of a tree and wondered if they took it. She saw a caterpillar and wondered if he ate it....

The story went on like that and ended with the girl finding her imagination in the form of a butterfly that fluttered next to her, whispering stories in her ear.

Sarah watched her teacher read it and then said, "I guess my imagination was playing Hide and Seek with me and I found it."

Her teacher smiled and said, "Sarah, you are right but it was the other way around. You were the one hiding, and your imagination found you."

Questions

How typical is Sarah?
How would most teachers feel about a student like Sarah?
What do you think of the teacher's response to Sarah's initial panic over the assignment?
What do you think might have happened if the teacher had not let the class go outside?

Why do you think the time outside resulted in Sarah's completion of the writing assignment?
What do you think the teacher meant when she said "your imagination found you"?

Comments

As educators we sometimes forget that environments convey silent messages to students about how they are expected to act in them. Schools are supposed to be productive places where every moment needs to be devoted to achieving objectives and outcomes. Some students have difficulty learning in this type of environment; educators often view them as having and/or causing problems.

Sarah, however, was the extreme opposite: she thrived in the school environment. Her success and her desire to sustain it became the very obstacle that prevented her from completing an assignment. Her motivation to succeed couldn't fill a blank sheet. The more she tried the harder it got and she panicked.

Fortunately, Sarah had a wise teacher who was in tune with her students. She read the look of panic on Sarah's face and knew that rational answers or explanations wouldn't diminish the emotion that had swallowed up Sarah. The teacher had faith in Sarah and the positive influence of time and the natural world on the creative process. Perhaps this aspect of learning, that recognizes the importance of being non-productive and reflective, is one that all teachers should value more and include in their classroom environment.

2

Social Emotional Learning

The district had made a significant investment in a social emotional learning curriculum. It was taught over the course of one semester in a health class for sophomores. Included in the curriculum were units on problem solving, decision-making, conflict resolution and bullying prevention.

The health teacher, Mr. Walsh, had been encouraged by how well the students seemed to enjoy the lessons. They read short scenarios of typical problems that students encounter in their lives. There were also videos depicting various dilemmas that students faced in a school environment. His students participated in animated discussions following the viewing. He reported to the principal that all of his students would easily pass the unit tests.

After the class had just finished their final lesson on the bystanders' role in bullying prevention, he gave them their homework assignment and dismissed them to go to their next class. The students filed out of the classroom door and after about half the students had exited the room, one student collapsed to the floor. The teacher hadn't noticed it because he was busy talking to a student. As the student lay there on the floor, the remaining eight students proceeded to step over him and exit the room.

Finally, the teacher looked over, saw the student on the floor and immediately signaled the main office to summon the school nurse. The student who collapsed had a history of seizures and fortunately suffered no injuries from his fall. Once Mr. Walsh was assured that the student was okay, he realized that almost half of his students had totally ignored their classmate. He was deeply troubled.

He met with the administrative team and together they viewed the whole situation on a video taken from surveillance cameras. Sure enough, they observed eight students watch their classmate fall to the ground and then proceed to step over him. They were shocked, dismayed and angered at the callousness of these students. They discussed what type of disciplinary actions to take but couldn't find anything in the Code of Conduct that these students violated. One assistant principal thought that they should receive intensive lessons after school on empathy and responsibility. Finally, Mr. Walsh suggested, before they made any decision, he would interview the students individually to find out why they were indifferent towards their classmate.

He interviewed the first student who stepped over the fallen classmate. She replied that the student who fell had a history of pranks and she didn't want to get fooled by him. The second student said that he was so surprised by what happened that he just froze and followed the lead of the girl ahead of him. The third student said that he wanted to help, but didn't know CPR and was afraid he would make the situation worse. The fourth student said she thought that the teacher would see it and attend to the problem. The fifth student said that he wanted to help but was afraid of missing his next class because his teacher penalized students who were late. The remaining three students also said that they felt that they should help, and felt bad about not helping. They stated that after seeing five students step over him, they figured that those students knew something that they didn't know, so they just did what the other students did.

Mr. Walsh reported the results of his interviews back to the administrative team. He shared what each individual student told him. In addition, he added that all of the students felt bad about what happened and guilty for not helping. The eight students said that it was the first time anything like that had ever happened to them and that if it happened again they would help. They all inquired about how the fallen student was doing and offered to apologize to him.

After hearing this summary of the interview, the principal asked the team for ideas on what to do. No one spoke up. They were still staring at the table deep in thought.

Questions

How does this scenario affect your thoughts about social emotional learning programs?

Why did the lesson on bystander behavior seem to have little or no effect on the eight students who stepped over their classmate?

Why did the faculty initially attribute the students' behavior to callousness?

Why did the faculty discuss disciplinary actions for these students?

What would have happened in the scenario if the students were not interviewed?

How legitimate were the reasons given by the students for not helping the student who collapsed?

Why do you think there was silence when the principal asked the team for ideas?

What are the possible implications of this scenario for schools interested in social emotional learning?

Comments

Social psychology refers to the fundamental attribution error as our tendency to attribute a person's behavior to some internal state or character trait. Human behavior is highly influenced by a variety of environmental conditions that affect how an individual perceives a situation and subsequently acts in response to it. Minor changes in the circumstances of the situation have a great influence on human behavior.

Therefore, we all have the tendency to make quick judgments (usually negative ones) when we try to infer the motivation and intentions behind a certain behavior.

The behavioral approach used in many of our schools, however, recognizes the pitfalls of trying to figure out what is going on a person's mind. To counteract this tendency, many behavioral interventions focus solely on behaviors that can be empirically observed and measured. In this scenario, however, the students' perception of the social environment greatly influenced their response to their fallen classmate. Relying solely on what can be observed might have required disciplinary interventions that would not have fit what the situation called for.

The idea of "what we see is **not** all there is" might make responding to student behavior more challenging, but educators who explore what they cannot see, i.e. what students are thinking, stand a better chance of responding to student behavior in a fairer and more effective way. What Mr. Walsh discovered via his interviews was how the students' perception of the situation affected their response to it: he needed to dig beneath the surface of what could be observed in the video.

The students in this scenario were able to explain their behavior, but this is not always the case. To complicate matters even more, very often a person's behavior is a mystery to that person because they are not consciously aware of how the situation triggered a particular response in them. What happens in these situations is that individuals "make up" reasons afterward simply because it is untenable not to know the reason.

Ironically, the silence of the faculty after they heard the students' responses is a positive sign. They should in the future be cautious in the judgments and conclusions they reach about students. Slowing down and reserving judgments to consider the context of a behavior should not be equated with not holding students accountable for their actions: that is a false dichotomy. Students can be held accountable for their behaviors. They will, however, be better equipped in the future to make better choices if adults help them to understand why they did what they did.

Time invested in proactively helping students understand their own responses to their social environment should reduce and prevent incidents of inappropriate behavior and promote pro-social behaviors.

3

The Red Vest

Lucas always wanted to be first. He wanted to be the first in line for lunch and recess. He wanted to be the first student to answer the teacher's question. But most of all, in the morning, he wanted to be the first student from his bus to go through the front door of the school.

Lucas felt happy when he was first and sad when he wasn't. The problem was that trying to be first usually got Lucas into trouble.

On the first day of the new school year, when his school bus was the first to pull up in front of the school, Lucas got very excited. He could be the first kid of the year and of the whole school, not just his bus, to go through the front door of the school. Wow!

Lucas, even though he was in fourth grade, sat in the front seat of the bus, so he could be the first student in line to get off. He stood on the top step moving his feet up and down like he was running in place.

The bus driver announced, "Have a great day" and opened the bus door. Lucas took two quick steps down and launched himself off the bottom step. He lowered his head and charged as fast as he could towards the front door … until he smacked into Principal Robinson.

Just as he was about to say, "Sorry," he heard Principal Robinson say, "Hey Lucas, I need your help this year." She reached into her pocket, pulled out a red vest and unfolded it. Then she reached into her other pocket and pulled out a sign that read, "Please Walk, Thank You."

Principal Robinson said, "Can you help me keep the kids safe by wearing this red vest and holding up this sign every morning and afternoon?"

Lucas smiled and said, "Sure, Ms. Robinson."

So from that day on Lucas was allowed to be the first student off his bus. He walked into school, put on his vest and held up his sign until all the kids were off the buses and in school. He did the same at the end of the day at dismissal.

Lucas never got in trouble any more for trying to be the first student in or out of school. But he still got in trouble for calling out in class and for pushing and shoving when he tried to be the first in line for lunch and recess.

One morning as he was standing in front of the school holding the sign and wearing the red vest, he got an idea.

Lucas went to Principal Robinson and asked, "Can I wear this red vest all day?" She replied, "Sure Lucas. Why not? Give it a try." And Lucas did.

When it was time to line up for lunch and recess, Lucas wearing his red vest walked over with the rest of the kids and got in line with no pushing or shoving. When the teacher asked a question, Lucas raised his hand and waited to be called. The red vest worked! But Lucas wondered why, so he asked Principal Robinson.

"Ms. Robinson, why does the red vest keep me out of trouble?" She replied, "The red vest just helps you do what you already know to do. It gives you a little nudge and that was all you needed."

Lucas thought about what she said and asked, "Could anything else give me a nudge?" Principal Robinson said, "What do you think?" Lucas looked serious and then his face lit up with a smile. He answered, "What about a red rubber band?" Principal Robinson replied, "Great idea. I have plenty of them in my office."

The next day Lucas put on the red vest in the morning and held up the sign, but after that job was completed, he took off the vest and put the red rubber band around his wrist.

When it was time to line up for lunch and recess, he tugged on the red rubber band and walked over with the other students. When the teacher asked a question, he tugged on it and raised his hand. The red rubber band worked. Wow!

After a few weeks of wearing the rubber band, he forgot to put it on. He still remembered to walk to get in line for lunch and recess. He still remembered to raise his hand in class. He still remembered to do his job with the red vest and sign at the beginning and the end of the day.

One day Principal Robinson saw Lucas walking to line up for lunch. She noticed that he didn't have the red rubber band on his wrist. She called him over to talk. Principal Robinson asked, "Lucas, you don't need the rubber band any more. You remembered on your own?" Lucas replied, "The red vest and rubber band didn't help me remember; they helped me forget." Principal Robinson asked, "Forget what?" Lucas smiled and said, "About wanting to be first."

Questions

Why was being first so important to Lucas?
Why did Principal Robinson have the red vest and sign ready for Lucas?
How did the red vest work for Lucas within the school?
What was the significance of Lucas having the idea to wear the vest in school?
How did Lucas's relationship to Principal Robinson affect his ultimate success?
How does this story of behavior change compare/contrast with other ones you have experienced?

Comments

Competition among students is often promoted in school as a motivation for achievement and reward. Lucas has internalized this lesson of school to such a degree that it gets him into trouble. This is why changing behavior can be so difficult: students get a mixed message about how they are supposed to act.

The default approach to changing student behavior has traditionally relied upon rewards and consequences. The reasoning behind this approach ostensibly makes sense. Most people want good things to happen for them and want to avoid negative things. Many students are able to make rational decisions about their behavior by thinking, "I want this to happen so I will act the way I am supposed to." The problem happens when students like Lucas don't *think ahead*. Increasing consequences either positively or negatively typically doesn't get them to *think ahead*. Most of these students know what is right and wrong but act impulsively without thinking. When this lack of thinking gets them in trouble (which they don't want) they can often feel that they have no control over their lives—not a good thing to learn.

In this tale, Principal Robinson had obviously been thinking about Lucas and his problems. She had probably tried the typical approaches to getting him to change and had been unsuccessful. Her decision to give him the red vest and sign reflected a fundamental shift in strategy for changing behavior that was based on the premise that identity drives behavior more than consequences. Lucas was given a new identity that was completely different from his previous one; this identity had behaviors that were incompatible with his old identity. Ironically, most students like Lucas are not given opportunities for developing new identities because their previous behavior typically disqualifies them from these opportunities. Lucas's experience of the new identity and the success that came with it was attributed to the red vest. He later transferred it to a red rubber band. This was a transition period for establishing a new identity. Once the new identity was established, it colored his entire school experience and changed everything for him—for the better.

4

The Lesson

Ava was a bright, energetic girl, and well liked by her classmates. She had a single mom and three siblings, so her family's financial situation was very different from her classmates.

Ms. Castelli, her fourth-grade teacher, had a soft spot in her heart for Ava.

Ava qualified for the free lunch program, but the cafeteria offered extra snacks to buy. Most students were able to bring in 25 or 50 cents a day to buy chips or ice-cream sandwiches. Every day, Ava had to watch her friends eat the snacks that she wanted to eat, but couldn't afford.

One day a student reported to Ms. Castelli that two quarters were missing from her desk. Ms. Castelli thanked the student for telling her. She gave her two quarters out of her own pocket and reminded her, in the future, to keep her money secure and out of sight. Although this student sat close to Ava, Ms. Castelli was reluctant to assume Ava took the quarters and decided to let the issue pass. Instead, without mentioning names, she gave a mini-lecture to the class about the importance of not leaving money in plain sight and respecting other people's property. She hoped that the problem would not happen again, but sadly soon enough it did.

While supervising the students in the hallway, Ms. Castelli saw Ava reach into another student's backpack pocket and take out two quarters. She stepped in quickly, took the money out of Ava's hand and gave it to the student, who probably thought that they had fallen on the floor. She sent the class to lunch and discreetly asked Ava to step into the empty classroom. Ava knew she was caught doing something wrong and started to cry.

Ms. Castelli commented on Ava's immediate remorse and gave her the opportunity to share her feelings. Ava said she was jealous of the other kids and wanted to have snacks too. Ava also confessed to stealing the money off the student's desk and repeatedly said, "I am so sorry." Ms. Castelli listened and thanked her for telling the truth and accepting responsibility. She called Ava's mother. And the three of them met in person to discuss the problem.

As a result of this meeting, Ava wrote a letter of apology to the students and pledged not to do it again. They agreed on a plan where Ava could stay after school a few days a week to help clean and organize the classroom, so she could earn money to buy snacks one or two days a week. For Ms. Castelli, the 50 cents a week was a small price to pay to resolve this problem and help a girl like Ava.

All seemed to be fine until April when the school held its annual book fair. Ms. Castelli worried about how this would affect Ava, who had to watch her peers buy books when she couldn't. She planned on contacting Ava's mother, so they could work out a way to avoid a replay of the snack money problem.

Before she could make that phone call, something happened that shocked and deeply troubled her: a five-dollar bill that she had put on her desk was missing. It was a Wednesday when staff chipped in and ordered lunch from the local deli. She typically took a five-dollar bill from her purse, placed it on her desk and returned the purse to her locked desk drawer. As much as she regretted leaving the bill on her desk even for a moment, there was no doubt that it was gone. Although she hated to think so, she concluded that Ava, who sat near her desk, was the student who took it. As she had predicted, it was the snack money problem replayed: Ava grabbed the bill so she could shop for books like the other kids.

She met with Ava and calmly and carefully told her what she thought happened. She said she could understand the temptation but there was never an excuse for stealing. Ava listened but denied it. Ms. Castelli tried a second time and Ava denied it again. Ms. Castelli told her to think about it and they would meet at the end of the day. Again, Ava denied it. Later Ms. Castelli called Ava's mother and asked her to try to get the truth out of Ava.

The next morning they met, and Ava once more denied taking the money. At a loss for what to do, Ms. Castelli thought about conferring with her principal and possibly the school resource officer. She didn't want Ava to think that she could get away with stealing. She reasoned it was better to frighten her a little now, than have her steal later in life when the consequences of being caught would be far more drastic.

Worried about what to do, Ms. Castelli had trouble sleeping that night. The next morning as she was putting on the same pantsuit jacket that she wore on Wednesday, she reached into her side pocket and felt the missing five-dollar bill. Now she remembered that she never put it on the desk. Instead she took the bill from her purse and put it directly into that pocket. How could she forget doing that? She suddenly felt sick to her stomach; it was probably the worst she ever felt as a teacher. How could she be so certain and be so wrong? How could she put Ava and her mother through that terrible ordeal?

So she met Ava as soon as she got off the bus, and apologized profusely to her. Ava seemed embarrassed and didn't say anything. She called Ava's mother and apologized to her. That was not enough: she publicly apologized to Ava in front of the class saying that she wanted them to learn the lesson that she learned about jumping to conclusions and falsely accusing people. Finally, at the end of the school day, she met with Ava again to apologize. Ava reached out and put her hand on Ms. Castelli shoulder and said, "That's okay—we all make mistakes."

Years later, Ms. Castelli received a letter with Ava's return address in the corner. She was surprised and happy to hear from one of her favorite students. Yet the sight of Ava's name still sparked a sharp pang of regret in her heart. When she opened the envelope there was a copy of an essay (with an A+

on it) that Ava had written for her senior English class. Attached to it was a small post-it note that said, "Dear Ms. C, I thought that you would like this essay. Thank you for ALL the lessons you taught me. Love, Ava"

As Ms. Castelli stared at the title of the essay, "The Person I Most Admire: My Fourth-Grade Teacher, Ms. Castelli," she felt a small tear roll down her cheek.

Questions

Why did Ms. Castelli have a soft spot in her heart for Ava?
What do you think of how Ms. Castelli handled the first missing money problem?
What do you think of how Ms. Castelli handled the second missing money problem?
How did the previous two missing money problems affect her response to the missing five-dollar bill?
What do you think of Ms. Castelli not involving the principal or the school resource officer?
Why do you think Ms. Castelli didn't believe Ava's denials?
What do you think of Ms. Castelli's reaction to her mistake of accusing Ava?
Why do you think Ms. Castelli was Ava's most admired person?
What lessons did Ava learn from Ms. Castelli?

Commentary

Teachers make mistakes. That is not surprising, especially when you consider just how many decisions they make each day. They are aware of some of their mistakes and are unaware of many of them. Because of the hierarchical structure of schools, most teachers are accountable to administrators or sometimes parents, but not to their students.

Teachers or those in leadership positions are sometimes reluctant to admit mistakes, especially to those they lead. They are afraid that they might appear to be less competent and therefore receive less respect from those they lead. All of these factors contribute to teachers being fearful of revealing that vulnerability.

Teachers and administrators can suffer from the *amnesia of leadership* because it is too easy to forget their own experiences of having less power and authority. The irony of this situation reveals itself when teachers complain about administrators in much the same way that their students might complain about them. Unfortunately, most teachers and leaders often fail to realize that revealing their mistakes or any area of vulnerability doesn't lessen students or followers' respect. In fact, admitting mistakes, doubts, and uncertainty in an honest straightforward manner only tends to increase respect and even more importantly trust. Although most followers want leaders that they can look up to, they also want leaders who have some degree of empathy or a sense of what it is like to be in their shoes. When students see their teachers make mistakes and admit them, they can feel that their mistakes are okay and will be more likely to admit and consequently learn from them.

With the example of Ms. Castelli, her empathy for her students and her willingness to admit her own mistakes created a high degree of psychological safety for her students. Her words and actions conveyed to all of her students key values of honesty and responsibility, i.e. she set a high bar of integrity. Students are more likely to strive to meet those standards when they feel that failure is an acceptable part of the process of attaining them. The combination of high standards of behavior and high levels of psychological safety ultimately provide the most optimal conditions for learning.

This was what Ava was conveying to Ms. Castelli when she wrote and shared her essay. As she grew older and gained more experience, she realized that her time in Ms. Castelli's room and its lessons helped her learn how to learn. Those lessons can be beacons of light that guide people throughout their lives especially when times are tough.

5

Robbie Remembers

It was the first day of the school year and Robbie, a third-grade student, had a lot on his mind. His family had moved over the summer and he was hoping his new school would be better than his old school.

At his old school Robbie didn't earn as many Spirit Bucks as the other kids.

Spirit Bucks were what the teachers gave to kids who remembered the rules: kids got caught for being good. Robbie forgot the rules: he got caught for **not** being good.

When he walked into his new school, he kept his baseball cap on his head hoping it wasn't against the rules. He walked past someone, maybe the principal, who didn't tell him to take it off. He looked around for a poster with the rules that he knew he would forget and another poster telling him how many Spirit Bucks he wouldn't earn *because* he forgot them. Robbie didn't see any posters.

As Robbie was walking down the hallway, he felt a tap on his shoulder. He put his hand on his cap and turned around. He saw an adult smiling at him and heard a friendly voice say,

> Hi Robbie, I have been waiting for you. I'm Mr. Rodriguez, the school counselor. I checked with your teacher, Ms. Reilly, and she said it was okay for us to meet for a few minutes. Let's go to my office. Okay?

Robbie didn't think he could say "No" so he replied, "Okay" and followed Mr. Rodriguez.

Robbie thought that Mr. Rodriguez would tell him the rules and how he could earn some new type of Bucks. So he was surprised when Mr. Rodriguez said, "We are so happy to have you with us. This is a very friendly school; there are a lot of exciting projects going on in third grade. You'll see."

Mr. Rodriguez continued, "So Robbie, tell me about your old school. How was it for you?" Robbie looked down at the floor and mumbled, "Not too good."

Mr. Rodriguez paused, looked around his office, took a nerf ball off the shelf and said, "You know what, Robbie, let's play a little catch." Robbie looked up and before he could say anything, he had to catch the nerf ball that was coming towards him. They played catch for a few minutes and Mr. Rodriguez escorted Robbie to his classroom.

At his next meeting with Mr. Rodriguez, Robbie talked about all the things he did wrong—all the times he forgot the rules: he yelled out in class, said swear words when angry, hit kids who made fun of him, forgot his homework, ran down the hallway, and a lot of other things he shouldn't do. Mr. Rodriguez just listened and wrote them down on a sheet of paper.

Mr. Rodriguez asked Robbie about the things he remembered to do in school. Robbie didn't say anything for a while. Mr. Rodriguez said, "Let me help you. Just answer "yes or no." Robbie nodded and said, "yes" to a long list of things: he hung up his jacket, took his book out when told to, read what was on the board, did worksheets, took books out of the library, said "thanks" to the lunch lady and many other things. When Mr. Rodriguez finished, he wrote the word, *"Remembered"* on top of that list and *"Forgot"* on the top of Robbie's list of the rules he forgot to follow. He asked, "Which list is longer?" Robbie pointed to the "Remembered" list

Mr. Rodriguez asked to borrow Robbie's cap. Robbie handed it to him. Mr. Rodriguez pulled apart the Velcro tab at the back and asked Robbie to touch it. He said,

Robbie, that's Velcro. Stuff sticks to it. You see our brains for some reason are like Velcro for the negative things. For the positive things, the list I helped you make, our brains are like Teflon; it's something very slippery. Things don't stick to it; they slide off. You do more positive things than negative things, but negative stuff sticks to the brain. We have to focus on the positive not the negative—that's the best way to move forward.

Mr. Rodriguez pointed to the "Forgot" list and said, "So, how does this sound? Let's pick one thing on the 'Forgot' list and figure out a way to move it to the 'Remembered' list. Sound like a plan?" Robbie chuckled and said, "Yeah, a plan."

Robbie picked "yelling out in class" as the first thing to move. Mr. Rodriguez coached him to count "one, two, three" silently in his head and then raise his hand. Robbie practiced this with Mr. Rodriguez.

In the classroom, when Ms. Reilly asked a question about a story, Robbie raised his hand and she called on him. Robbie blurted out "one, two, three" like it was the answer. Ms. Reilly smiled and said, "Good try, Robbie. You got part of it right—raising your hand. Next time, just count in your head."

The next day Robbie reported what happened to Mr. Rodriguez who said, "You are moving in the right direction—that's what counts." After about a month of practicing with Mr. Rodriguez every morning, Robbie moved three things from the "Forgot" list to the "Remembered" list.

One morning Robbie, as usual, went straight to Mr. Rodriguez' office but no one was there. Robbie didn't know what to do but waited for a few minutes. Mr. Rodriguez walked through the door, saw him and said, "Oh Robbie, I am so embarrassed. I am so sorry. I was talking to the principal. I should have remembered our meeting but I just **forgot**." Robbie stared at him, made a face like he was angry, but then smiled and said, "That's okay Mr. Rodriguez, nobody's perfect." Mr. Rodriguez chuckled and bowed to Robbie. Then they fist bumped and the two of them ended up laughing for what seemed like a long time.

Questions

Describe Robbie's identity (how he viewed himself) in his old school.

Why did Robbie immediately put his hand on his cap when he felt the tap on his shoulder?

Why did Mr. Rodriguez decide to play catch with Robbie after he said, "Not too good"?

Why do you think Mr. Rodriguez used Robbie's cap to tell him about how the brain works?

Why would it be important for Robbie to know about how the brain worked?

Why did Mr. Rodriguez ask Robbie to point to the longer list—the "Remembered" one?

What was the significance of Robbie picking the item to move from the "Forgot" list to the "Remembered" list?

How did Mr. Rodriguez and Ms. Reilly work together?

Did Mr. Rodriguez deliberately forget his morning meeting with Robbie or not? Why? Why not?

Comments

Positive behavior programs are certainly an improvement over punitive and reactive approaches to discipline. For students like Robbie, however, the presence of rewards for positive behavior presented opportunities for him to perform worse than his peers. Robbie walked into his new school wondering "who" he would be in this new environment and consequently was on the lookout for any sign that would tell him.

Mr. Rodriquez was attuned to Robbie's need to establish a positive identity. He interacted with Robbie in a way that presupposed that Robbie wanted to succeed and do well. Robbie's problems in his previous school were not the result of his lack of motivation to do well; there were other reasons at play.

Mr. Rodriquez supported Robbie in creating and sustaining a different identity in school: a positive one that could make mistakes and correct them without shame. He empowered Robbie to understand how his brain works, to recognize the positive, and build on it by self-selecting a goal and achieving it. Mr. Rodriguez was successful because he didn't just tell Robbie what to do, but tangibly guided him through the process of making progress. Mr. Rodriguez's experience as a counselor probably told him that feeling in charge of one's life was the best motivation for succeeding.

6

Character Education

Trevor and his friends typically walked as fast as they could to claim the back seats of the bus. When they got there, Trevor made sure he sat on the aisle. Unlike his friends who joked around, he didn't say a word. He was too busy watching the rest of the kids to make sure they stayed out of fifth-grade territory.

They all did except one boy. A third grader, with a baseball cap pulled down to hide his face, had dared to cross the invisible border. Trevor popped up, planted his feet in the aisle, and flipped the boy's cap off his head. The boy looked up and saw Trevor's fist hovering an inch away from his chin. Trevor looked down into the boy's face and yelled, "Get outta here, NOW!" In one quick motion the boy spun around, snatched up his cap and retreated to the third-grade section of the bus.

Trevor sat down again. His friend, Mark, tapped him on the arm and said, "What's wrong with that jerk? Doesn't he know the rules?" Trevor leaned back in his seat and folded his arms. "He does now. They all do."

For weeks, Trevor didn't have to be mean or yell at kids because they stayed out of the back.

Then one day something changed. Mikey, a kindergarten student, moved into Trevor's neighborhood. Trevor liked Mikey; he was a neat kid. That weekend they discovered they both liked baseball and played catch together.

So on his first day going to school, Mikey followed Trevor down the aisle to the back of the bus. Trevor turned around and calmly said, "Mikey, not here. Go sit in the front." Mikey said, "Okay," and waved to Trevor just before he sat down with the other kindergarten kids. Later, on the ride home, Mikey tried following Trevor again to the back of the bus. This time Trevor quickly turned around and snapped, "Mikey, get back," pointing to the front of the bus. Mikey said, "Okay," and walked up the aisle again.

When they got off at the same bus stop, Trevor said, "Mikey, you can't sit in the back with me—it's against the rules." Mikey just smiled and walked home.

But the next day and the day after that, it kept happening: Trevor saying, "Get back" and Mikey saying, "Okay." Trevor thought that Mikey had made up a silly game, like playing catch-back and forth, back and forth.

He wondered how long Mikey would keep playing it.

The other kids started to wonder too.

One morning on the bus, Stephen, a fourth-grade student, turned around and said to Trevor, "Don't worry. We'll teach him the rules." Stephen and his friend Josh smiled at Trevor, giving him a thumbs-up sign. Not sure of what they meant, Trevor slightly nodded back at them.

When the bus pulled up to the school, Trevor noticed that Stephen and Josh rushed to get off the bus with the kindergarten students. As Mikey stepped off the bus, Stephen pulled Mikey's lunchbox out of his hand, sending it tumbling to the ground.

Before Mikey could pick it up, Josh kicked it like a soccer ball. Because it looked like an accident, other kids started kicking it too. Mikey scrambled around trying to grab it. Each time he came close, another foot kicked it away.

When Trevor finally stepped off the bus, he saw Mikey's lunch box spread open with a sandwich and thermos still inside. He saw baby carrots (some rolling around and some crunched flat) and the crumbs of stomped-on chocolate chip cookies being swept away by the wind.

Trevor also saw Mikey, with a scraped knee showing through the hole in his pants, crying on the ground. As he went over to him, he heard Stephen and Josh call, "Hey Trevor." He glanced at them standing by the door of the school showing him the thumbs up sign again. Then he felt sick to his stomach.

By then Principal Fisher, who had been greeting students, rushed over to check on the situation. As she arrived she saw Trevor crouching down next to Mikey.

Trevor zipped open his own backpack, took out a bag of baby carrots and a granola bar and said, "Here Mikey, take these. I don't need them for lunch. I have other things to eat". Mikey put them in his lunchbox and snapped it shut. He stopped crying and stood up.

Principal Fisher took Mikey's hand. She looked at Trevor and said, "Trevor, you were a Good Samaritan. Thank you so much for helping Mikey and sharing your lunch with him. You should be proud of yourself. I will take over from here. You can go to your classroom."

Trevor didn't talk too much for the rest of the day.

At home he asked his parents what a "Good Samaritan" was. They told him the story from the Bible and asked him why he wanted to know. Trevor said that Principal Fisher called someone a Good Samaritan and he wondered what it meant. Trevor went to bed but had trouble sleeping.

At the end of the month, the school held an assembly featuring the character trait for that month. On stage Principal Fisher proudly announced that Trevor was the recipient of the Character Award for Kindness. She relayed the story of how he helped another student in need. Trevor went on stage to receive his certificate. He accepted it from Principal Fisher and rushed off the stage as fast as he could.

Later that afternoon, after dismissal, the school custodian, as he was about to empty the trashcan, looked inside, paused for a moment, and brought it over to Trevor's teacher. Pointing to what caught his eye, the custodian said, "This is odd. Why would a student do this?" The teacher looked in and saw that the Kindness Award certificate with Trevor's name had been ripped up into pieces. She shook her head, looked at the custodian and said, "I have absolutely no idea."

Questions

What does Trevor's vigilance about the back of the bus tell you about him and the bus environment?

When Mark, Trevor's friend, asks if the third grader knows the rules, what are the rules he is referring to? Where did they come from?

What does Trevor mean when he says, "they all do"?

What motivated the fourth graders, Josh and Stephen, to knock Mikey's lunchbox out of his hand?

Why did Trevor feel sick to his stomach?

Why do you think he didn't mention to his parents that the principal praised him for being a Good Samaritan?

Why did Trevor rip up and throw away his award certificate?

What do you think of the reactions of the custodian and the teacher to the ripped-up certificate?

Comments

Students and staff live in the same time and space, but inhabit completely different worlds. Each world has a set of social norms very specific to their social environment. Although these norms are never explicitly stated, they exert a very powerful influence on how people treat each other—more influential than rules and consequences.

The school bus is one place where students can interact without adult authority directly supervising them. Although the bus driver has authority, his/her primary responsibility is to safely drive a bus full of students. At best, he/she becomes aware of only the most blatant rule violations.

Think of the bus environment as a *Lord of the Flies* situation on wheels, with its own set of rules determined by the social hierarchy of the students.

Trevor and his fifth-grade friends had earned the right to the back of the bus. They had risen to the top of the social hierarchy. Trevor, who was probably a top student and a model citizen in school, was also at the top of the bus hierarchy and took his job very seriously. The fourth-grade students, who were next in line to assume the top positions, wanted to impress those currently in charge, Trevor and his friends. This explains why they targeted Mikey though they probably had nothing against him personally. They observed Mikey giving Trevor a tough time and wanted to help and impress him. When Trevor came off the bus he felt bad for his young friend. When he saw Stephen and Josh giving him the thumbs up, he realized that he held some responsibility for what happened to Mikey.

In the world of adults, Trevor deserved the award for kindness, yet in the world of students, Trevor committed mean and hurtful acts. The students on the bus who experienced life under the reign of Trevor saw him being held in high esteem by adults who were in charge in the school environment. Younger students, therefore, were given all the more reason to emulate his actions in every environment.

Fortunately, Trevor had a moral compass that gave him a different message about right and wrong, one that made him reject the award from adults who were out of touch with what really happened. A greater concern would be if Trevor had accepted the award and learned to accept the external interpretation of what is right and wrong, i.e. that gaining status and approval supersedes moral values.

7

A Buddy and a Pal

Jason liked his red hair and freckles until he saw William and Jessica whispering to one another on the school bus. Later at the lunch table, they announced to all the fourth graders, "Hey look, Jason's hair is so red, he looks like a rose—a rosebud." Jason felt every kid staring at him and heard someone say, "Look—his face is getting redder." From then on kids would walk by him and whisper, "Hi, Rosebud."

Jason wished his hair were blond, brown, or black: any color but red. And for a pencil that could erase every freckle from his face.

He wondered what to do. Tell his teachers? They would tell him not to tattle. Tell his parents? They would call the school, making things worse. Tell his best friend, Ryan? He would think he wasn't tough enough to handle it.

So he wore a baseball cap pulled down to his ears to hide his hair and face.

But one day the whispers stopped because "Rosebud" turned into "Buddy." Now kids he didn't know would call out, "Hi, Buddy." No one could ever get in trouble for calling someone "Buddy" when it meant friend. But any kid who called him "Buddy" was not his friend.

It felt like "Buddy" was written in black permanent marker on a nametag that was stuck on him with superglue.

So he tried to escape from hearing it. He said he felt sick at recess so he could go to the nurse's office. He asked to go the bathroom as many times as he could at lunchtime. And he made sure he was the last kid on and off the school bus. But he still heard "Buddy" every day from the kids.

At least it was only kids.

But one day as Jason was going down the steps of the school bus, Mr. Lewis, the bus driver, said, "Have a good day, buddy." Jason froze and felt his face get warm. He turned around and stared at Mr. Lewis. "I am not your buddy. Don't call me Buddy. My name is Jason."

Mr. Lewis replied, "Whoa. Just trying to be friendly." Jason looked down and said, "Sorry, Mr. Lewis for yelling at you. It's not you. It's those other kids."

Mr. Lewis said, "What happened?" Jason told the whole story of the whisper and how "Rosebud" turned into "Buddy" and how his whole life was now ruined. Mr. Lewis said, "Yep. They sure pushed the right button on you. I've seen it hundreds of times—it's happened to me too."

Jason asked, "What do you mean, *button*?" Mr. Lewis said, "Well, everybody's got a weak spot—something that really bugs them. It's like you got a button on your chest that says, *"Push this and you will drive me crazy."* He pointed to one of the buttons on Jason's shirt and said, "Kids find out what bugs you and when they do, they push it and you get upset and angry. And each time you get upset, they push it more."

Jason nodded. He imagined the word "buddy" being a finger that poked his button. "What can I do?" he asked.

Mr. Lewis replied, "Well, Jason, what would make you stop pushing a button?" Jason said, "If I pushed it a lot and nothing happened, I guess I'd stop after a while."

Mr. Lewis said, "Yup. That's one way. What if you pushed a button and expected a light to go on and the room got darker—the opposite of what you wanted? That's another way to stop it." Jason shook his head saying, "Right now, the button works—my feelings just come out."

"Yeah, but once you know about a problem, you can have a plan to solve it. Practice helps too!" replied Mr. Lewis.

"But how do I practice?" asked Jason.

Mr. Lewis replied, "Here we go. "I'll call you 'Buddy' and you take a breath and say, 'Thanks, pal' ... Let's try. Ready. ... *Hi, Buddy*." Jason started to get upset, but took a breath and mumbled, "Thanks, pal."

Mr. Lewis said, "Let's do it again."

They did it ten times in a row. Each time Jason said "Thanks, pal," his voice got louder. They practiced five more times and Jason laughed as he said, "Thanks, pal."

Mr. Lewis nodded, "Jason, see your button's not working—it's doing the opposite. It's making you smile when it is supposed to get you upset or angry." Jason imagined a sign under his button reading "out of order."

Mr. Lewis said, "Homework assignment: tell your best friend and even your folks about this. Practice with them. The more practice the better."

Jason did his homework. By the time he came to school the next day, he must have said, "thanks, pal" over 100 times.

When he got on the bus, Mr. Lewis winked at him and whispered, "Hi Buddy." Jason smiled and said, "Thanks, pal." Mr. Lewis gave him a thumbs-up.

Jason walked by William and Jessica. They shouted out, "Hi Buddy. How you doing, BUDDY?" Jason felt like he wanted to punch them but the words, "thanks, pal" automatically came out of his mouth. Then the smile they had on their faces vanished.

Jason reached out to them for a fist bump. They put up their fists in slow motion and Jason bumped them a little harder, but not much harder, than a friendly fist bump. He said, "Thanks. My buddy and my pal."

That was it—they never called him "buddy" again. After that Jason heard some kids call him, "Buddy", but it didn't bother him. His button was "out of order" for good; he was Jason again.

But he still heard "Buddy" one time every day. When he got on the bus in the morning, Mr. Lewis winked his eye and whispered, "Hi, Jason, my buddy." Jason would smile and reply, "Hi, Mr. Lewis, my pal."

Questions

Why do you think William and Jessica announced that Jason looked like a rosebud?

How would William and Jessica react to being accused of bullying?

Jason felt he couldn't tell anyone. How typical was his reasoning?

Why would Jason being called "Buddy" be considered bullying? Why wouldn't it be?

How was being called "Buddy" affecting Jason's ability to learn?

Why did the bus driver calling Jason "Buddy" provoke the reaction it did?

Mr. Lewis decided to coach Jason. Was this the correct decision? Why? Why not?

How could this situation have been prevented from happening in the first place?

Comments

Bullying can hide in plain sight. It can be camouflaged as friendly banter. It can be joking when said to one student and the same words can be piercing to another. These are just a few of the reasons why bullying is such a challenging problem in schools. It is totally unlike other incidents of inappropriate behavior that schools have traditionally confronted.

Students can learn to be effective and clever in bullying other students for a few laughs or simply to "flex their muscles" demonstrating their influence over peers. Students who end up as targets of bullying can feel that admitting this to adults will further stigmatize them and probably make the situation worse. Therefore, they have to figure out how to escape the situation on their own and typically fail.

Jason was fortunate to have a friend in the bus driver who used his common sense in helping him. The bus driver wasn't concerned about correctly identifying bullying or following the right protocol in addressing it. He wanted to help a student in need and use his own life experience to do so. We don't know what would have happened if Mr. Lewis's coaching hadn't worked, but at least Jason no longer felt like a victim. He also realized he had an ally who could help him use a different strategy in the future, if he needed to. Perhaps Mr. Lewis's approach, however, has implications for how other educators can approach the challenging problem of bullying.

8

X Marks the Spot

The whole situation had been bothering Melissa for quite a while. She had trouble sleeping because of it. Recently she started to question what every other kid in ninth grade just took for granted: Robert was a jerk, a pest that no one liked. Melissa had to admit that she didn't like him either.

Robert said stupid things at the wrong time. He dressed sloppily. He bumped into people and never said, "Excuse me". He was usually late for class. Melissa tried to ignore him. Some kids didn't ignore him; they enjoyed taking shots at him and getting laughs at his expense.

Sometimes Robert was oblivious to the put downs, but sometimes they got to him. He would react by yelling out a swear word and a teacher would hear it. Robert got in trouble, not the kid who had teased him.

One day Melissa, after she finished track, got on the late bus to go home. After a few stops, the only two kids left on the bus were Melissa and Robert, who were sitting across the aisle from one another. Robert had a sketchpad on his lap and was busy drawing pictures. He had stayed late because of detention. Melissa had never seen Robert so focused and on task doing anything. She decided to slide to the aisle seat to take a closer look at what was absorbing Robert's attention. She noticed a series of cartoon panels. If she hadn't seen Robert working on it, she might have thought that it was a comic book that you would buy in a store.

She summoned up enough courage to say, "Hey, that looks pretty cool, can I take a closer look?" Still looking at the sketchpad, Robert instinctively snapped back, "Bug off! None of your business." Melissa didn't reply. Robert looked up and saw that Melissa still looked interested. With a slight smile, he looked at Melissa and said, "Well, if you really want? Here." He handed Melissa the pad. Melissa said, "Thanks." The panels depicted a superhero rescuing the planet. When Melissa finished reading it, she said, "Wow. This is great!"

As she handed the sketchpad back to Robert, she sat next to him. Before they knew it, they were talking about movies, TV shows, favorite books and even their favorite foods. For Melissa it was like she was meeting a new student—not the same old obnoxious Robert that she had known since kindergarten. She thought, "I could be a friend with him." When the bus pulled up to Robert's stop, they looked at each other, neither of them knowing what to say. Then at the same time, they said, "See ya around."

Melissa felt a knot in her stomach. What would happen if she started talking to Robert in school? She thought about the times she laughed when one of her friends made a joke at Robert's expense. She knew it was wrong, but she couldn't help herself especially when her friends were laughing too.

Later that night, Melissa lay in bed replaying the last ten years of being in school with Robert. The more she thought about it, the worse she felt. How could Robert come to school? She couldn't if she was teased and put down every day. What a mess, a terrible mess this whole situation had become.

Her mind kept searching for a moment when this mess started, but she realized that it had always been this way.

She did remember, however, one moment in first grade. The principal was walking next to her as her class was going back to their room after lunch. Up ahead, she saw Robert kicking the bottom of the wall, like it was a silly game to show he could kick and walk at the same time. The principal was nice, so Melissa felt okay talking to him, but she didn't say "hi." Instead she reported what she witnessed, "Robert is kicking the wall." The principal looked at her and nodded. He seemed to be in a hurry and quickly disappeared down the hall. Lying now in bed and remembering this scene in her mind, Melissa wondered why she tattled on Robert when he wasn't hurting anyone.

Suddenly it came to her. She was only doing what she thought she should do. She was doing her job: what her teacher would want her to do. As early as first grade, Melissa knew that Robert was different from the rest of the kids and not in a good way. Robert was doing things that the teacher didn't like. Robert was a troublemaker; he made things worse for the rest of the class. Melissa, the teacher and the rest of the kids were on the same team, not Robert: us against him. The principal was on this team, therefore, he needed to know what Robert was doing, so Melissa reported it.

Melissa realized that as early as first grade, everybody, the teachers and students, thought that Robert only got the treatment he deserved.

As she lay in bed, she imagined Robert walking down the hallway in front of her. She noticed a small black X on his back. As the years passed and Robert grew taller, the X grew bigger. By high school, no one could see Robert; he was no longer Robert. He had become an X: a target so big that it invited kids to take all the shots they wanted.

She searched in her mind for a way to help Robert and erase the X on his back. Yet even as she stared into the darkness of her room, she worried that the X was made with a permanent marker.

Questions

Why was Melissa troubled about Robert even before she had the encounter with him on the bus?
How aware do you think staff members were about the social dynamics involving Robert?
How come some students couldn't resist taking shots at Robert?
How did being on the bus alone with Robert affect Melissa?
Why did Robert initially rebuff Melissa's attempt to connect with him?
Why did the moment in the hallway stand out in Melissa's memory?

Why did it take so many years for Melissa to gain insight into why Robert was treated the way he was?
How aware were others in the school about Robert's artistic ability?
Why did Melissa think that the X on Robert's back might be permanent?
What could the school do to change the situation or correct the mess?

Comments

Bullying doesn't wound students. It pours salt in a wound that already exists. The wound is the pre-existing condition of not belonging, of being negatively perceived as different or not as good as everyone else. This wound makes a student like Robert vulnerable to mistreatment. Robert and the other students sadly have accepted his status as a given in their current situation. Whether what happens to Robert is considered bullying or not, is beside the point: his school experience has been a daily reminder of his low social status and how he doesn't belong.

Melissa's moral compass tells her that something is wrong with the whole situation. She is troubled by her own attitude and behavior but when she looks around it seems like she is the only one who is. The problem is that she might not be; there could be other students like her. Other students could be silenced by their fear of the consequences of challenging the status quo. They all know the risks of daring to call attention to the injustice that seems to hide in plain sight of everyone including the adults.

The greater problem is that the school environment has engendered this situation in the first place, when the first-grade class perceived Robert as a troublemaker. Young children naturally want to please their teacher and gain approval, therefore, when Robert acted in a way that displeased the teacher the other children naturally wanted to align themselves with their teacher. Sadly, this "lesson" made Robert a target for mistreatment; he was someone who deserved some form of mistreatment. He needed to be mistreated in order for him to learn and follow the school rules.

In her search to find the origins of how Robert lost his true identity as a person and gained his target identity, Melissa realizes her own failure to see Robert as a person and her contribution to Robert's identity as a target. Melissa is left at the end of the story knowing that this injustice must be confronted and corrected. This situation, her complicit role in creating and sustaining it and her doubt about changing it, deeply worries and saddens her.

9

The Slur

For Ryan, a junior at Rockport HS, it was the straw that broke the camel's back, or better yet, in his mind, it put the final nail in the coffin.

What happened to him proved once and for all that the school he attended wasn't really **his** school—it was just a building he went to every day along with a 1000 other kids.

He admitted that some kids probably felt differently about the school. These kids were the ones the teachers liked: good at sports, or got high grades, or always followed the school rules, or better yet did all three.

But Ryan knew the other side of these kids. He saw them when the teachers weren't looking.

A lot of them drank and did drugs when they were out of the building. These kids thought they were better than other kids and let everyone know that they were better. They got off on the fact that they fooled the teachers into believing they were the type of kid that all students should be like. These kids seldom got in trouble. And if they did, guess what? The teachers and principals were quick to give them a second chance—they got off with no punishments.

What bothered him the most, however, was how mean they could be to the kids who weren't like them: Ryan and kids like him. They were just the butt of jokes, which were daily reminders of their low status.

Ryan had concluded that this whole terrible situation was because he, and the few friends he had, shared one thing in common: they were just average. And being average in Rockport HS really *sucked*.

Here is the incident that removed any doubt in Ryan's mind, and that proved his point about Rockport HS being just a building and NOT his school:

He once got in trouble for something he never did. He was sitting in class listening to a boring social studies lecture and he heard over the loud speaker, "Ms. Toomey, would you send Ryan Doyle to Ms. Baxter's office." He was shocked to hear his name because she was the Dean of Discipline and he hadn't done anything wrong.

He got up anyway and went to her office. As soon as he sat down, Ms. Baxter looked at him and said, "Who do you think you are? Blowing off detention. Don't you have any respect for the rules of this school? You were caught stealing snacks from the cafeteria. Don't you know that you could get arrested for stealing?" Ryan was stunned. He didn't even like the stupid snacks they had in the cafeteria.

When he didn't respond immediately, Ms. Baxter said, "Don't sit there with that phony innocent look on your face. That's disrespectful." Ryan finally spoke up. He remembered that there was a Brian Doyle in his class who bragged about stealing snacks, so he replied, "Maybe you have me mixed up with Brian Doyle. I am Ryan Doyle." Ms. Baxter looked down at her desk at a list of names and then she said, "You aren't Brian Doyle?" Ryan replied, "My name is Ryan." Ms. Baxter, looking a little perturbed, mumbled, "I guess there is a mix-up—I have the wrong Doyle. You can go back to class." She didn't even look at him. He waited for her to say something more. He got up and went back to class.

That was the straw and the nail—that was it for him and Rockport High.

A few days later, when Ryan read in the paper that a few racial slurs were heard at a basketball game, he wasn't surprised.

There were more and more kids moving into his district from a neighboring city. These kids were from minority groups: non-white kids. A lot of these new kids were better at sports than the kids the teachers liked. These new kids were also a lot cooler to a lot of the girls.

If Ryan and his friends were second-class citizens, these new kids were even worse—they were invaders. The kids the teachers liked definitely did not like these city kids and didn't want them there.

These racial slurs (called out by who knows whom) at the basketball game caused quite a mess. The newspapers had the story on the front page. There were local TV reporters stationed outside the building trying to get students to comment on the situation.

The superintendent vowed to get to the bottom of this problem. He announced to the school that the district would have zero tolerance for any form of racism or disrespect. Within days he convened a task force and before you knew it, the district had a new slur policy banning and prohibiting any type of language that disrespected anyone. Anyone who violated this policy would suffer serious consequences.

Ryan thought that the whole situation was a total farce. Where was the policy protecting him and his friends from the kids the teachers liked, and from people like Ms. Baxter, the Dean of Discipline?

Ryan decided to get even and teach the school a lesson once and for all. He wrote a note using cut-out letters of different sizes and shapes from a magazine. The note simply said: **Make Rockport High White Again! Non-whites go back to where you belong!**

He put the note in an envelope and printed an address label to put on it, so his handwriting couldn't be detected. He mailed it to Ms. Baxter at the high school.

He smiled when he imagined how the scene would go: Ms. Baxter bringing the note to the principal and then the two of them bringing it to the Superintendent. They would walk in and hand him the note. The Superintendent would look at it and shout: "What the f ...?" and then slam his fist on his desk.

Ryan sat back and waited for the next flurry of news stories to appear.

He also waited for the day when he could leave Rockport HS forever.

Questions

How accurate was Ryan's perception of how the teachers viewed students in the high school?

Why was having the teachers' approval so important to Ryan?

Why would being "average" generate the feelings it did in Ryan?

What was Ryan waiting for Ms. Baxter to say to him after she realized the mistake?

What do you think of the Superintendent's efforts to solve the problem of slurs?

How correct is Ryan to think that the slur policy is a "total farce"?

What do you think the district will do in response to the note?

How likely is Ryan to get away with writing and sending that note?

Comments

A central question that every school should ask itself is: are we a community or a group of people who just happen to be together in the same place and time?

Yet this question is seldom asked in schools, especially in schools like Rockport High School that typically graduates over 90 percent of its students and sends most of them to good colleges.

Fortunately, Ryan's strategy of revenge for feeling inferior and undefended was not a violent one. However, his motivation for setting off this PR bomb could be considered similar to ones that posed physical threats. Probably a more likely scenario, than the one depicted in this tale, is that a student like Ryan bides his time, goes through the motions of going to school and in the future will never attend any type of alumni event.

Schools fortunate enough to never experience acts of violence or vengeful non-violent ones, are faced with a challenge: accept the status quo or actively seek to find out if their school is a community, and if it's not, then do something to make it a community.

4

Teacher Tales

1

Invisible Learning

Ms. Rollins thought that she had it down to a science: give her six weeks and she would have even the friskiest class of kindergartners eating out of her hand. Her tried and true bag of tricks kept them in check, on task and under control.

It all started with getting the class to "crisscross applesauce" as a cue for sitting in a circle the right way. Once they were settled into this posture, she had an extensive menu of routines and call and response songs to get the children clapping, marching and chanting while following her lead.

For example, she had a song to teach the Days of the Week. She would point in rhythm to the word for each day as the students sung them. From the days of the week, she moved to the months of the year and the number representing that date. She also had a routine for checking the weather every day.

Following this practicing together, she would randomly call on a student to come up, get the pointer and re-enact the whole sequence of events. If the student hesitated or looked confused, Ms. Rollins would announce, "Who wants to help _____?" And she would call on another student to give as much or as little of the answer as that student needed.

So practiced were the students in these routines that behavioral problems had little room to grow. For those exceptional times when a student wasn't attending, following directions, or was talking to a peer without permission, Ms. Rollins would first give a stern, no-nonsense look that students quickly learned to interpret as a sign of impending trouble. If that didn't correct the situation she said their name in a tone that matched her look. She would then quickly shift her tone and facial expression to praise a student who was doing what was expected: catching that student being good.

When this predictable sequence didn't correct the situation (which it typically did) she used a time-out chair prominently situated off to the side of the circle. Students were given three seconds to correct their behavior before they were told to sit in the chair until she gave permission to return.

All in all, Ms. Rollins loved being a kindergarten teacher. She was grateful that she didn't have to put up with the defiance that her colleagues talked about with students in higher grades. The only real down side of her job was dealing with the administrators/principals (in her school usually a new one every two years) telling the same old story about the students not doing well on their state assessments, particularly language arts, in grades 3–5.

She acknowledged this problem because most of the students were from lower socio-economic backgrounds. Her job was to provide them with what they were lacking in many of their home environments: order, predictability, structure and a respect for authority. Once she established those, then the students could focus on academic skills. Although she kept this analogy to herself, she viewed herself as a trainer breaking a wild horse that resisted having a rider. In the same way, she was getting her students under control for her colleagues to take over from her.

To her, the district's "flavor of the year" i.e., a new program designed to raise test scores and get the school off the state's list of *struggling schools*, was an annoyance and a waste of time. She didn't need a new initiative imposed from above to tell her how to do her job.

Cooperating with her district's mandate on collecting data, she assessed each student individually twice a school year. She called students up one at a time to sit next to her desk so she could ask them to identify letters, sounds, and sight words. On these days, she had little choice but to give the rest of the students free play time. Materials, primarily toys, blocks, play dough, etc. that were typically kept out of students' reach and sight were made available to them.

So on an assessment day very late in the school year, Principal Davis, popped into her room unbeknownst to Ms. Rollins. The students were involved in a wide range of activities. One small group of students handed him a piece of paper and asked if he would write down the words for their restaurant menu: hamburger, pizza, fries, chicken nuggets, etc. He happily obliged and became their first customer. Principal Davis joined another group of students who had constructed an elaborate series of buildings made out of various kinds of blocks. This was the scene of an accident and fire that required the assistance of police cars, ambulances and fire trucks. The students made sound effects and created dialogue for each of these crews. Another group of students were using markers, crayons, scissors and glue sticks to create greeting cards. They asked him to help them write messages to their family members.

Principal Davis, who had never heard this *buzz* of expressive language and excitement coming from this room in any of his previous visits, felt uplifted by the energy he felt from the students. So with a smile still lingering on his face he approached Ms. Rollins. She was surprised to see him. With a playful frown, she looked at him and said,

> I'm sorry you wasted a trip here. I should have told you that nothing would be happening today because I had to do these individual assessments. Come back tomorrow when I will have my usual lessons and you will see some real learning happening.

Questions

How competent was Ms. Rollins as a kindergarten teacher?
What were her expectations for her students?
How do you think she would have been as a teacher of older students?
What do you think about her reaction to the professional development initiatives of the district?

What do you think of the district results on language arts tests?
What was her attitude towards play?
What do you think of her analogy to training horses?
Why was the principal happy to see the children playing the way they did?
Why do you think Ms. Rollins gave the principal a "frown" when apologizing to him?
Why do you think Ms. Rollins viewed play as "nothing happening"?

Comments
This tale asks a fundamental question: what is teaching and learning in school? Ms. Rollins puts a big emphasis on controlling her students. She teaches them to follow directions and the rules and to respond to what she says. She is very successful in teaching what she considers the fundamentals for success in school. Her thinking goes like this: students need to be controlled in order to learn and can learn only what they are taught.

She is bothered by administrators, who point out that students in her district are not gaining the skills they need in language arts, i.e. reading, writing, speaking and listening. She has difficulty seeing a connection between the lack of opportunities she offers for students to think, talk and interact with each other and poor test results later on in language arts.

The challenge a teacher of young children faces is how to balance the need for order and predictability with children's natural curiosity and need for social connections. Perhaps Ms. Rollins needs to reflect more about learning before being so certain about teaching.

2

The Unlikable Student

Michelle had been teaching middle school social studies for three years. For her, teaching was a mission not a job. Many of her students had difficult backgrounds and walked through the classroom door with many needs. Michelle embraced the idea that she taught "students" first not just social studies.

Michelle tried to connect the concepts contained in the curriculum like justice, equality, freedom and democracy to the students' lives. Her students sat in clusters of four desks so they could talk to each other about the ideas and concepts of the curriculum. She took to heart the idea that a goal of education was to develop responsible citizens.

Starting with her first year of teaching, she had quickly learned not to take the words and actions of students personally. She kept her emotions in check and her focus on learning, instead of getting caught in the power struggles with students that she heard her colleagues complain about. This was why she avoided the faculty room during lunch periods: she didn't want to hear negative comments about students. Instead she ate alone with one or two other like-minded teacher friends. She also invited several students to eat lunch with her in the classroom on a weekly basis.

Michelle was proud of how she kept her ideals and avoided becoming jaded or even cynical like some of the other teachers in the school. This was the reason why she was so distraught over her third period class. She had invested so much time with them in building community. She had the entire class sit in a circle so they could see each other's faces and hear their ideas. She made sure that the students found something in common with each other, knowing that even these simple things in common built relationships. All of these strategies worked with her other classes, but her other classes didn't have Jason.

Jason wasn't overtly disruptive and kept his words and actions well within the limits and expectations of the school and classroom. In many ways, Jason reminded Michelle of the cynical teachers that she tried to avoid. Like those teachers, his cynicism in the form of snide remarks or facial expressions affected everyone in the social environment. Sometimes she wished that Jason were more openly defiant and disruptive because then she could feel justified in seeking help and support from the school counselor or the administration. Given the everyday crises and problems that those people encountered, her complaints and issues with Jason would seem like nothing.

She tried inviting Jason to eat lunch with her, but he continued his sarcastic comments and detached manner even when he was alone with her. She asked him to volunteer for different jobs in the classroom, and he did so, but he never shed his sarcastic attitude. Deep inside, Michelle wished Jason would move away; she was relieved on the few days when he was absent. Michelle hated this about herself and believed that this was the type of attitude that eventually would lead to the same cynicism that afflicted so many of her colleagues. Despite all of this, Michelle maintained the same pleasant face and tone of voice in all of her interactions with Jason: she wasn't going to give in to what she considered her darker impulses. She kept them to herself.

There was one person, however, who heard about Jason on a daily basis, her husband, Michael. Fortunately, he was not an educator so their conversations didn't end up as just shoptalk. He listened without offering techniques or suggestions and Michelle was glad for that. Most of the time he didn't say anything more than "I am sorry you have to deal with that."

One night, however, he said something different, "I know that this Jason situation is weighing heavily on you because you love your students and want what's best for all of them—*especially* Jason." Michelle suddenly became quiet and felt tears welling up inside of her. Michael noticing this, asked, "What did I say? I'm sorry." Michelle remained silent almost afraid that speaking would lead to tears.

After this moment of silence, she took a deep breath looked at her husband and said, "I don't love Jason, I don't even like him. He drives me nuts and I feel like yelling at him and telling him how he is ruining my classroom AND MY LIFE." She paused and suddenly felt like a 1000-pound weight had been lifted from her shoulders. She whispered to Michael, "I don't like Jason."

She went to school the next day ready to face the same issues in third period as she did the day before, but for some reason, she didn't dread seeing Jason walk through the classroom door. Jason was Jason and she was at peace with not liking him; she would teach him what he needed to learn and that would be it.

But something did change: she started to notice other things about Jason beside his snide and sarcastic comments. It wasn't anything dramatic. She noticed him giving another student a pencil. She noticed him interacting with some students who were not very popular. She noticed him smiling at times when he wasn't just reacting to what she was saying but rather interacting with his classmates. Obviously, Jason hadn't changed and probably had done similar things before but she just didn't "see" them.

For her part she didn't think that she treated or interacted with Jason any differently than before, but she noticed that he was reacting differently to her. There were times when his sarcasm stopped and he seemed invested in the class discussion. Jason changed and she really didn't how or why.

Somehow within a few days, third period began to seem like every other period.

After two weeks of this *change,* one night at dinner, her husband joked and said, "I miss Jason. What happened to him? Did he move away?" Michelle sat back, smiled and said, "No, he didn't but maybe I did."

Questions
What do you think about Michelle's attitude towards her job?
What do you think about her deciding to stay out of the faculty room?
How do you think the rest of the faculty felt about her?
How come she couldn't learn not to take Jason's words and actions personally?
Was she correct in not seeking help for her problem with Jason? Why? Why not?
Why do you think her strategies with Jason didn't work?
What's the significance of her stating, "I don't like Jason"?
Why do you think she was able to start seeing things she never saw before in regards to Jason?
Why do you think Jason changed?
What do you think Michelle meant when she said that maybe it was *she* who moved away?

Comments
Our greatest strengths can also be our weaknesses. Michelle's great strength was her determination to maintain her ideals. She had very high expectations for herself and her students. She didn't want the culture of the school to change her.

This sense of mission and her high expectations *worked* for her and her students until she met Jason. Jason forced her to confront the limits of her idealism. He was a threat to her on many levels: a student she couldn't win over, a student who seemed to have as much influence on the class as she did, and perhaps a sign that her more jaded colleagues might have been right all along. Jason evoked an aspect of herself that she didn't like and couldn't accept.

Teachers are expected to care for students. Even teachers who complain about students and treat them harshly claim to care for them. The reality, however, is that teachers are human beings interacting with other human beings. The emotions that flow out of those interactions cannot always be positive.

Fortunately, Michelle had a husband who was a good listener and his honest response to her allowed her to see her own blind spot existing in her heart and mind. Once she could see her blind spot, and could name it and accept it, it had less power over her. Ironically, once Michelle confronted and accepted her limitations (not being able to love/like all of her students) she was able to see Jason in a different light; he became less of a threat to her. Perhaps Jason sensed that she was trying to change him, and did his best to subtly undermine her. Once Michelle was freed of her need to make Jason into a more acceptable student, he sensed her acceptance and changed his behavior even if he wasn't aware of doing so.

3

The Good Old Days

In the future, technology had evolved to the point where children could easily acquire the basic skills of reading, writing and mathematics at home. By the time children were five years old, their reading skills had developed as a natural outgrowth of their ability to speak their native language, as well as a second or third language. For example, as children looked at the objects in the world and learned to utter that word, they would also see the printed word superimposed on that object.

With every home equipped with such technology, parents could easily teach their children what they would learn in elementary school requiring less time than the traditional six years (K-5). Virtual reality technology had also allowed children to visit foreign countries, to travel back in time to historical events, and to experience problems requiring mathematical problem-solving techniques. In addition, the knowledge readily and instantaneously available on mobile devices, made libraries and books less and less necessary.

As part of this technological evolution, society began to question the purpose of schools, which were now becoming childcare centers. Faced with this existential problem, policymakers analyzed the benefit of having children together in physical locations outside of their home environment. They decided that schools should change their purpose to teaching children how to interact and relate to others.

Schools would become places where students could experience cooperation and sense of community. Places where students could learn the social skills of self-regulation, problem solving, conflict resolution; consensus building and the basics of citizenship. Developing and mastering these skills became the basis for their comprehensive curriculum and instructional program.

Since teachers no longer needed to teach academic skills, teacher education and professional development focused on understanding human development and social psychology. If some children lacked academic skills, parents were expected to use available technologies to ensure that their children would learn what they needed to attend school, so they could benefit from the social and emotional learning that filled their school day. The overall outcome and benefit of making this dramatic and comprehensive shift in curriculum and instruction would be a less violent and more harmonious and democratic society.

This dramatic shift in education after several generations became the norm: students learned academics at home and came to school to learn how to get along with others. The teachers who had learned to teach academics had either retired or passed away. All was well. Schools had regained their status as a necessary institution for society. And just as the literacy rate in the later days of academic schools was over 90 percent, students now graduated high school with a universal set of social and emotional skills. The "EQ" of America had dramatically improved.

But slowly things began to change, more and more students started entering school with gaps in their academic skills. These children were a small minority but there were enough of them to warrant considerable time and attention on the part of educators. Schools had special programs to help those students who didn't acquire the self-regulation or problem-solving skills of their peers, but there didn't seem to be anything in place for students with gaps in their academic skills. Some teachers naturally were able to integrate academic instruction into their curricula, but many teachers seemed to be at a loss for how to do that.

For example, role-playing various social scenarios was a common instructional strategy. Students would be given scripts to read and act out. They had to read about the characters they were supposed to portray in these scenarios, so if students had shaky reading skills, they were at a serious disadvantage in mastering the required skills of the curriculum.

Across the country the increasing rate of students with academic needs spurred the development of academic reading and math programs that many schools started to fit into the busy school day. It was unclear who was qualified to teach these skills, but all teachers ultimately would have to take responsibility for teaching the "whole child."

More and more principals had to stand in front of their staff on the first day of school each year and announce that their district had mandated a variety of academic programs that needed to be incorporated into the school day. Some teachers embraced the idea, however, many others had serious doubts that they kept to themselves. After grudgingly accepting the imposition of these extra programs, many teachers would gather in parking lots filled with driverless electric cars. The conversations they had were an animated mixture of complaining about having too many things on their plate and longing for the time when parents taught their children how to read, write and do math, or what they longingly considered as the good old days.

Questions

Do you think it is possible technology could one day allow children to learn the basics of elementary education at home? Why? Why not?

If so, would that be a good thing or bad thing for our society? Why? Why not?

If schools could primarily focus on social/emotional skills, would it lead to a more peaceful world? Why? Why not?

What do you think about the idea of adding programs/curricula to address problems in school?

Why do teachers often keep their doubts to themselves in meetings?

Did the *good old days* ever exist? Why? Why not?
Why do many teachers long for them?

Comments

Technology has had a profound impact on how the great majority of people live their lives. People communicate differently, shop differently, receive entertainment differently, travel differently, and view the world differently.

Technology in education has impacted schools in how they perform many logistical tasks such as grade keeping, attendance taking, communicating to parents and communicating among teachers. These changes, however, are in most cases peripheral to the heart of education: what occurs in the classroom.

Walk into most schools and high impact technological changes would not be too noticeable. The basic structure of how classrooms function has remained stable even if an electronic white board has replaced a blackboard. Although technology has been embraced and used effectively in many schools, there are still educators who view it as having a negative impact on students by fracturing their attention, lessening student engagement with subject matter and impairing social skills.

Traditionally there has been clear line that could be drawn between learning to get along with others and learning academic skills. As a result of this bifurcation, most educators have conceded that most students learn academic skills at different rates and therefore support students who struggle in this domain. The same acceptance has not been made for students who struggle to navigate the social/emotional world. Whereas deficiencies in academics are addressed through remediation and special education, deficiencies in social/emotional skills are typically addressed by the behavioral approach using rewards and punishments.

This futuristic scenario flips the entire perspective on the purpose of education on its head. Regardless of whether such a scenario becomes true, educators must confront an ever-growing need in our culture for helping students learn to get along with each other. Is the answer to this problem adding a curriculum, program or new strategy? If not, what would constitute a more productive approach? Could such a discussion foster a deeper and more thorough exploration of the purpose and function of education in our culture?

4

Under the Table

Ms. Anderson was worried about what the new principal would think of her. Her colleagues felt the same way. Would he be the type of principal to pop into her class unexpectedly? She had tenure and really didn't need to worry. She knew she was a good teacher. She had been teaching second grade for five years and felt confident in her ability to instruct and help students learn their academic skills. If asked where her weakness lay, she would freely admit it was dealing with non-compliant students.

At a faculty meeting, Principal Collins announced that he liked to pop into classrooms. He assured the staff that his visits were to connect with students, not to check on teachers. Ms. Anderson was a little worried about this because of Josh, a new student whose family had recently moved into the district. His parents had warned her that Josh had some difficulty in first grade following directions. He had always been an anxious child; they thought that it might be because he was adopted.

The school year, however, was off to a good start. Josh did fine for the first week: he followed directions, got along with his classmates, and did his homework. Ms. Anderson had started to think that she had a great class and the year would be a rewarding one for everyone.

All that changed one day when she was teaching a math lesson and tried a new questioning method. She told the class, "I am going to try something different—this time, no raising hands. I have your names on these popsicle sticks and I will pick one out of this cup and call on that student to answer." As she was shaking the can of sticks and about to pull one out, Josh dashed out from his seat and went and hid under a small worktable on the side of the room.

Ms. Anderson continued teaching as best she could, trying to ignore Josh, but the other students weren't—their eyes were fixed on him. Before she could think of what to do or say next, Principal Collins opened the door, walked in and sat in a chair towards the back of the classroom. Ms. Anderson almost swore out loud but stayed calm, at least outwardly. Principal Collins saw the students looking under the table at Josh, but then they shifted their attention to him. He said, "Ms. Anderson this looks like an interesting math lesson. What are we learning today?" She replied, "I think our students can tell you." Principal Collins called on the students who raised their hands to tell him about the lesson. The lesson proceeded as planned, but Josh stayed under the table. Thankfully for Ms. Anderson, lunch was next on the schedule.

As soon as the lesson was over, Josh crawled out from under the table and returned to his seat. Ms. Anderson didn't say anything to him but directed the whole class to line up to go to lunch. They all did, including Josh, who acted like nothing had happened. She brought her students down to the cafeteria, but when she returned, Principal Collins was still in her room sitting at the same table that Josh hid under.

When she saw the principal, she felt her face grow warm and sat down at the table. She decided to take the initiative and apologize for the lesson he had just observed. To her surprise, Principal Collins replied, "I thought it was a wonderful lesson. Didn't you?" Ms. Anderson was surprised but said, "But what about Josh?" Principal Collins said,

> Oh yeah. I guess we'll have to figure out what's going on with him. That might take some time. Maybe you should schedule some time alone with him, to get to know him one to one. After a while you could talk about how he is feeling and how come he went under the table.

Ms. Anderson felt a tremendous weight lifted off her shoulders. She thanked the principal and said she would do what he suggested.

After a few one-to-one meetings with Josh, he told her that he didn't like the can with the popsicle sticks. She explained why she used it and gave him permission (as she would later give to all the students) to say "pass" if she called his name and he couldn't answer the question. After that conversation, Josh never went under the table again.

Questions

Why does a new principal create anxiety in teachers?
How common are Ms. Anderson's feelings about herself as a teacher?
What does it mean to have a great class and rewarding year?
Do those two things always go together?
Why did Josh hide under the table?
What do you think Ms. Anderson was going to do before Principal Collins popped in?
Why do you think the principal asked the question he did?
Why did he ignore Josh?
Why do you think Principal Collins didn't seem as concerned about Josh as Ms. Anderson did?
Why do you think she felt a tremendous weight lifted from her shoulders?
What do you think about the principal's advice? Why do you think it "worked"?
What do you think Ms. Anderson and Josh learned?

Comments

A teacher needs to feel in control of a class. Losing control is perhaps the primal fear of most teachers. Teachers tell themselves that they *should* be able to keep their class and all their students on-task and engaged in every lesson. Competent and confident teachers set a high bar for managing and accounting for the wide range of behaviors that students can demonstrate during lessons. Experienced teachers have a so-called bag of tricks that they use to prevent inappropriate behavior and respond to it when it does occur.

Most conscientious teachers are also their own harshest critics. This is a double-edged sword for their professional growth: they take responsibility for improving their skills to meet new challenges, yet by doing so they run the risk of becoming too discouraged and negative about themselves.

Successfully managing their emotions as they face challenges is a skill that teachers can develop. This *emotional curriculum* for becoming a competent teacher is often hidden and unarticulated. As a result, it is easier to focus on a technique or strategy than it is to reflect upon how feelings and emotions affect how teachers view and manage their own professional development.

When it comes to emotions, however, adults have a lot in common with children. In many ways, Josh and Ms. Anderson are in the same boat emotionally. Both are having to contend with the unknown of having someone in authority evaluate their performance in school. Both want to please that person and gain that person's approval. Josh because he hasn't yet learned to control and/or hide his emotions, reacts to the fear of being called upon to answer a question he might get wrong. That is a risk he cannot bear, especially since he does not know how his new teacher will react. That uncertainty and the fear it generates triggers his flight response. If Ms. Anderson, therefore, reacts by getting angry and tries to force him to come out, it will only confirm his worst fears about her.

Ms. Anderson probably wishes she could escape her situation of having the Principal observe her incompetence as evidenced by one of her students being under a table. She keeps from swearing and doesn't run and hide when Principal Collins arrives unexpectedly.

Principal Collins helps her in two important ways: he gives permission for her to ignore Josh and continue with the lesson and he re-frames the situation from being a teaching failure to a problem with a student who needs to be understood. Principal Collins also points her in the direction of focusing on trust and relationship building rather than figuring out a trick for getting him not to go under the table or one for getting him out. Since the power dynamics of school often cast behavior problems as contests of control, teachers sometimes need to be re-directed to relationship building and trust as a starting point for addressing student behavior problems.

5

The Perfect Scenario?

In the future a pharmaceutical company developed a drug to help children attend better, control their emotions and ameliorate their learning problems. The drug had no apparent negative side effects and had been approved for human trials.

The company selected a school whose demographics closely matched those of the country. The company wanted to evaluate the effectiveness of the drug and needed two classes that were very similar. They also wanted to gauge teacher reaction to the use of the drug.

They found two teachers with similar years of experience and comparable levels of competence as determined by evaluations and student test scores. They selected two third-grade classes located next door to each other. All the parents agreed to have their children try the medication that would be administered once a day immediately upon the students' arrival at school. The students were told that they were taking a vitamin that would help them stay healthy. The teachers were given that same explanation for why the students were taking a vitamin.

As usual, both teachers had done a lot of preparation for the beginning of the year. They did their typical get-acquainted activities and both classes were involved in developing the class rules of the year. The two teachers often worked collaboratively and had prepared similar approaches for the start of the school year.

From day one, the students followed directions without being told a second time. They attended to all the lessons and completed all their assignments. After a few days, these two teachers compared notes on their classes. Both said that they crossed their fingers that the rest of the year would go as well as the first week. And that was exactly what happened.

When it came time for unit tests, since students attended so consistently, all passed easily. All the students consistently received a B grade or above on their assignments. The parents, who of course knew about the drug, honored the confidentiality clause and did not inform the teachers about it. Parent–teacher conferences, therefore, went very smoothly. By the end of October, both teachers shared with each other how thrilled they were about their classes and how well the school year had gone.

Fearing professional envy from their colleagues, the two teachers were guarded when they were asked about their classes. They replied that it was a good year so far and that was about all. In the faculty room during lunchtime, they would hear the stories of their colleagues about the typical ups and downs and struggles that came with teaching. They offered their support and advice as they had done in the past.

Both teachers continued to work diligently on their lesson plans. As they typically did, both teachers stayed at school past their contracted hours. They both went home tired but not as exhausted as they had been at times in the past.

As the end of the school year approached, one of the teachers thought about asking if she could loop (stay with her class for another school year) with her students. The other teacher, however, began thinking about the following school year and what a new class of students would be like. All of the students did well on their standardized tests and both teachers received excellent ratings on their evaluations.

Finally after the last day of class, the teachers were called into the principal's office and met with representatives of the pharmaceutical company. The teachers were told about how the "vitamin" was really an experimental drug. The reps thanked them for their contribution to their research. They were asked if they wanted to be involved in the trial for the following year and have their students continue to take their "daily vitamin."

One teacher smiled and said,

> Are you kidding, who in their right mind wouldn't want another year like this? This was my wish come true. I was able to teach like I had dreamed of, with no nagging behavior issues. I was able to stick to my lesson plans as I designed them. I covered every topic in the curriculum for the first time in my career. I went home every night feeling good about the day and was able to give my time and attention to my family. Sign me up for next year and every year after—I could teach for another 20 years if I could keep having years like this last one.

Then the other teacher spoke,

> I wish I had known this from the start. I feel that you have stolen a year of my career. Sure there was less stress or no stress but to be honest, I was bored to tears. I found myself envious of my colleagues when I heard stories of their struggles in the classroom. I felt like I was learning nothing as a teacher and that anyone off the street could have come in and taught the class. I missed driving home from school thinking of what I could do differently the next day to help a student or improve a lesson. My husband said he missed hearing my "war stories". Sure, I had more time and energy for my own children, but they sensed that something was missing with me—as if I had lost my identity as a teacher. My own kids liked hearing stories of what happened in the classroom. No! This was not a good year for me. If my students or all students end up taking this drug, I will resign my job and look for a different career.

Questions

Is it out of the realm of possibility that such a drug could exist? Would society benefit from such a drug? Why? Why not?

How do you think the parents felt about their children's year?
How do you think the students would feel about taking such a drug? Would their view change as they got older? Why?
What do the reactions of both teachers tell you about how they view their jobs?
Why did the teacher who stated she would resign initially feel so positive?
How are problems viewed in schools? In our culture and society? In our own lives?
How does this tale relate to teacher statements like, "I have a good/bad class this year"?
How many teachers in your school would feel like the first teacher? The second teacher?
How would these differences in attitude affect how the faculty could work together?

Comments

We have all heard the statement: be careful what you wish for. Since no such drug currently exists and the perfect scenario never becomes a reality, many teachers may continue to long for one like it. How does wishing for something that is not currently possible affect how a person does a job? How many teachers are consciously aware that they are waiting for the perfect scenario?

It is human nature to want life to be easy and problem-free, especially when we are surrounded by problems and stress. Our culture, as represented in advertising, however, continues to promote the idea that such a life is possible and attainable. How does the idea of the perfect scenario affect our acceptance of what is currently experienced?

Teaching can give someone a great sense of control; a sense that is very difficult to achieve outside of school. Should attaining this sense of control be what teaching is all about? How much do teachers have to learn from their daily experience with students? These fundamental questions about the mission and purpose of teaching, and learning are seldom pondered. What could be the benefit of asking and discussing these types of questions?

6

Data-based Decision Making

Jonathan was a junior who had just barely passed all of his subjects since freshman year. This was frustrating for his teachers because he had so much potential and he was a likable and friendly kid. Although he never qualified for special education services, Jonathan had received various types of support in school: afterschool homework help, peer tutoring and frequent meetings with school counselors.

Since the finals were just a few months away, his teachers decided that they should meet and review his progress. They agreed that they needed a common intervention and that they should be on the same page to deliver the right message to him.

The assistant principal, Ms. Percy, who knew Jonathan well and shared these concerns, facilitated this meeting. Each teacher presented data on his academic work: test scores, number of assignments completed and samples of his written work. They reviewed his discipline records and attendance records. In addition, subject area teachers had a turn to give their own assessments of Jonathan as a student including his strengths and his needs.

After they had each made their statement, the assistant principal asked the teachers to offer any ideas they had for helping Jonathan be more successful in school. His social studies teacher, Ms. Winston, spoke first,

> Of all the data that we reviewed, the most important piece of information that we cannot ignore is the fact

> that he has been absent an average of 1–2 times per week. He is missing 20–40 percent of instruction time—how could even the brightest kid succeed with that rate of attendance? I don't think he really cares that much about school and is not too motivated to succeed.

All of the teachers agreed that his attendance was a priority for their plan. Ms. Winston continued,

> I volunteer to meet with him and share the data with him. He needs to face the facts and the consequences of missing school so much. We should create an intervention plan where participation in extra-curricular activities is contingent upon improving his attendance. We can offer incentives like gift certificates to McDonald's. We should also inform him that on the days that he doesn't show up at school, our attendance officer will go to his house to investigate why he is absent. I can meet with him on a weekly basis to review the data on how he is doing.

Most everyone's head nodded in agreement and Ms. Winston said she would go ahead and write up this plan. As Assistant Principal Percy was about to wrap up the meeting and give the final okay for the plan, Ms. Lopez, the language arts teacher, spoke up,

> I know Jonathan and I know his background and family history. He has a lot on his plate at home: his mother has health issues, he has four younger siblings including a two-year-old sister, and his father, who goes missing for long periods of time. I know you can't argue with the data but I see it differently: given what he has to deal with, I admire how he is able to come to school 60–80 percent of the time. You could look at his attendance and academic record and see a deadbeat or you could look at it and see a hero. I recommend that we choose the hero.

There was silence following Ms. Lopez's remarks. The AP waited for the team's response. She finally said, "Should we design a plan for him? What would work?" They continued to think when finally Ms. Lopez spoke up again:

> Maybe instead of writing up a plan for him, we should ask him what he thinks, ask him what would work for him and how we could best help him succeed. I believe he wants to succeed. He probably has some good ideas for how we can help him.

Questions

How does Jonathan's profile affect how teachers view him?
What role does data play in determining an intervention plan?
Is there a tendency to think data provides a more objective way of addressing an issue? Why?
If Ms. Lopez hadn't spoken up, how likely would it have been for the team to agree to Ms. Winston's plan?
Why do you think that the first interpretation of the data emphasized the negative?
What do you think about the inference made about Jonathan's motivation for school? Did it make sense? Why? Why not?
Is Ms. Lopez making excuses for Jonathan and not holding him accountable for his behavior?
Which interpretation of Jonathan's data would lead to creating the most effective intervention plan?
Why is including Jonathan in the discussion so important?
Why do you think many schools overlook including students in developing plans to address the problems they are experiencing?

Comments

By the time a student is in secondary school, his/her identity as a student has been established in the minds of their teachers. Unfortunately, this identity can be projected onto the student and the student then conforms to it. This becomes a self-fulfilling cycle with the student then providing evidence or data that only proves that the identity is "true". Educators perceive students through a lens, but don't know that they do. Because of this they fail so see how the lens colors everything they see. This is a very human phenomenon and creates a very difficult cycle to break.

Edward Deming said, "Without data you are just a person with an opinion." Educators, realizing the truth of that statement, have rightfully embraced data as a way of getting a better assessment on what is actually happening in school environments. The problem, however, is that no data set can directly dictate a particular course of action. All data is subject to interpretation and is subject to confirmation bias for supporting a pre-existing opinion. Data sometimes can be an impediment for changing minds and producing an effective intervention.

Data in decision-making can also lead to groupthink: the tendency of a group to easily go along with a decision that appears to make sense and is quickly supported by most of the members of the group. Welcoming different or even contradictory interpretations of the data might slow down the decision-making process, but this turns out to be an essential component of insuring that an effective intervention is selected by the group.

Since students are at the mercy of how those in authority view them, educators cannot be too careful in making up their minds about them as students and as people. Ms. Lopez therefore was using the *data* she gathered from talking with Jonathan about his home situation and suggesting that additional data be sought from Jonathan. Educators must be open to all sources of data, including student voices.

7

Journey of a Chair

Among the laundry list of things to cover at the first faculty meeting of the school year was a plea to help the school custodian, Mr. Green. The budget cuts had left him without an assistant to help at the end of the school day. Since sweeping the linoleum-tiled floor in each classroom was an essential task, Mr. Green needed the teachers to train their students to put their chairs up on their desks at dismissal time. If students could complete this one daily chore, Mr. Green's job would be so much easier.

Ms. Carney and Ms. Draper were two first-grade teachers with neighboring classrooms. They were friendly and respectful of each other but had very different teaching philosophies and styles.

As they left the first faculty meeting together, they agreed that getting their students to do this simple task every day would be a challenge. Students can be in a hurry, especially at the end of the day, plus there were many other things to do at that time. Although they agreed it was a challenge and on the necessity of instilling this habit, they didn't discuss how they would do so.

The district had been promoting a positive behavior program, but left it to each teacher to decide whether or not to implement it in the classroom. Ms. Carney had some previous success with this type of approach She decided to use a marble jar intervention designed to promote whole group cooperation. At the end of the school day, if all the students remembered to put their chairs up on their desks, she would put five marbles in the jar, if not all but over half did, she would put in three marbles. By Thursday, if there were 15 or more marbles in the jar, the class would have an extra ten minutes of free play at the end of the day on Friday.

During the first two weeks of the school year, Ms. Carney had the class practice their end of the day routines, and by the end of the first month of school, the class was consistently earning their free time on Friday.

It continued this way until April of the school year, when the students started to forget. Ms. Carney thought that maybe it was the nice weather, their eagerness to go outside or that the extra free time on Friday was less motivating, but for the first time, the marble total fell below 20. Ms. Carney talked to the students about it. Following their talk, there were some weeks when they earned it and some weeks when they didn't.

Ms. Carney wondered how something that had worked and seemed so well established was now not working the way it had. It wasn't a big deal in the scheme of things, but it did puzzle her.

So it was with some hesitancy that she approached her neighbor, Ms. Draper. Ms. Carney stood in the open doorway of Ms. Draper's room and said, "Knock, knock. Got a minute? I need to ask you something." Ms. Draper pushed a chair out and motioned for Ms. Carney to sit. After commenting on the student artwork on the wall, Ms. Carney said, "It might seem a little silly at this point of the school year to be talking about putting the chairs on the desks, but I need to know how your students are doing with it."

Ms. Draper pointed to the chairs with their legs up in the air on the top of the desks and said, "It seems like they remembered today." Ms. Carney replied, "My students were remembering every day until a few weeks ago. How could they get the habit and then lose it? That's what I don't understand." Ms. Draper smiled and said, "My students forget too, but they are pretty quick to remember when they line up at the door." Ms. Carney nodded, "At this point we shouldn't have to be reminding them." Ms. Draper said, "I'm not the one reminding them, he is," and pointed to a large photo of Mr. Green above the classroom door.

> They see him, rush back to their desk and put their chair up. Sometimes a student will tap the student who forgot and point to the photo; when that doesn't work, I point. On rare occasions, I might point and say "Remember Mr. Green."

Ms. Carney had to admit the photo was a good idea; one that she would try. She wondered if it was just the photo that did the trick, so she said, "I could see some kids looking at the photo and thinking, 'so what?'." Ms. Draper replied,

> Oh, I don't think it's the photo alone. It's connected to the class meeting we had on the first day of school. I invited Mr. Green to visit our classroom and sit in the circle with us. He accepted the invitation and explained to the students how he needed their help. He also said that when they picked up their chair and put it on their desk, they were also making the school a better place. That seemed to be all that was needed. In January, I put up the photo for the one or two students who started to forget.

Ms. Carney had to admit the meeting was a good idea, but felt that she had to share how her marble strategy worked pretty well too. Ms. Draper listened without responding. Finally Ms. Carney said, "Well, we tried two different ideas and both worked. Bottom line is the chairs get up on the desks—that's all that really matters in the end. It doesn't make much difference how they get up there, does it?"

Ms. Draper replied, "I don't mean to be contrary, but to me **how** they get up there makes all the difference in the world."

Questions
Why didn't the two teachers discuss how they would get their students to pick up their chairs?

Why do you think Ms. Carney's students started to forget to put their chairs up on the desk?
Why did the teachers wait until April to share how they were doing with getting the chairs on the desks?
Why hadn't Ms. Carney noticed Mr. Green's picture on the wall?
Why did Ms. Carney say that both ideas worked?
Why does how the chairs got on the desk mean so much to Ms. Draper?

Comments

Schools are filled with many mundane chores for both teachers and students. Sometimes the list of things to do for teachers seems to leave little time for thinking about and discussing issues related to actual teaching and learning. The teachers in this tale were handed a mandatory chore to add to the challenge of teaching first-grade students. Ms. Draper and Ms. Carney were competent professionals who heeded the call to support the custodian and also knew that it wouldn't be easy.

This tale involves two interrelated issues: professional collaboration and motivation. The very physical arrangement of the school environment reflects the idea that teachers are independent operators. Ironically, the more competent and experienced a teacher is, the less likely that teacher is to collaborate with a peer. As result, it is commonplace that two completely different classroom cultures can co-exist without the respective teachers being aware of how they differ. The goal of getting a group of young students to consistently remember to put their chairs on their desks might seem insignificant (maybe that is why the teachers didn't discuss how they were going to do it), but it could be an accurate indicator of the classroom culture.

Ms. Carney's approach of using extrinsic rewards to motivate her class is difficult to criticize. Academic subjects, in the hands of a competent teacher, can be taught in an intrinsically motivating way, but boring, routine or even tedious chores are by their nature non-intrinsically motivating. Ms. Carney was wise enough to use the goal of putting chairs on desks to build group cooperation: the class had to work together to gain free time where they could socially interact. Her strategy worked so well, that she didn't need to check in with her colleague until the students started to forget—in April!

Ms. Draper's class faced the same challenge but right from the start she took a very different approach. She saw a clear connection between the task and a person: it wasn't something that just needed to be done, but something that helped someone. She transformed the completion of a mundane task into an aspirational goal for helping a real person. Students met Mr. Green and heard his request for help and for making the school a better place.

When an aspirational goal is tied to a simple, easy to perform action, most people become motivated to achieve it. The students in Ms. Drapers' class weren't putting their chairs on their desk to get the reward that the teacher had power to bestow, nor were they doing it to get something for themselves, they were doing something important for a person and their school. Ms. Draper realized that there was a deeper, more important lesson for the students to learn at the end of the school day. Hopefully the exchange between the teachers might prompt a very productive professional discussion.

8

The Mistake

Mrs. Wilkins had been teaching third grade in the same classroom for almost 30 years in the only elementary school of this small rural town. She had seen many staff, including principals, come and go.

She was a fixture of the town. Her husband was a retired mayor of the town. Her sister was the town librarian, whose husband owned the local bank and was president of the board of education.

Mr. Montgomery had been the school principal for two years. He was well liked and respected by the students, parents and staff. He realized that he had many veteran staff members, like Mrs. Wilkins, so he demonstrated due respect and appreciation for the school before he tried to suggest any changes or introduce new ideas.

Mrs. Wilkins had very few behavior problems and if she did, she handled them herself. She had high standards for her students both academically and behaviorally.

One of her students, Jessica, was a very bright and precocious child. Her parents had moved to the town from a nearby city when Jessica was in first grade. They did so because they wanted a smaller and less hectic environment in which to raise their family.

Jessica was very popular with her classmates and had no problems in first or second grade. She did not, however, get off to a good start with Mrs. Wilkins. It wasn't anything dramatic or serious. For example, Jessica often raised her hand to answer before Mrs. Wilkins could finish her question. Mrs. Wilkins calmly corrected Jessica whenever necessary, but she was concerned about the influence Jessica seemed to be having on the other children.

There was one habit of Jessica's that bothered Mrs. Wilkins: Jessica would smile whenever she observed another child being disciplined for any reason. Mrs. Wilkins hoped that this habit would eventually stop but it hadn't by the middle of the school year.

One day, Mrs. Wilkins asked a question during a math lesson. She ignored Jessica's shaking hand and instead called on Joshua, who had not raised his hand. Joshua had been daydreaming and gave an answer that was totally disconnected from the question. Jessica burst into laughter and yelled out the correct answer. Mrs. Wilkins looked sternly at Jessica and said, "Stop that laughter and take that smile off your face." Jessica quickly put her head down and stared at her desk.

Thinking she still detected a slight smile on her face, Mrs. Wilkins quickly walked next to Jessica's desk. "Look at me," she demanded. Jessica kept looking at her desk. "LOOK AT ME, NOW!" Mrs. Wilkins repeated. Jessica seemed frozen unable to move and kept looking down at her desk. Giving up on getting her to look at her, Mrs. Wilkins now demanded, "Stand up and apologize to Joshua." Jessica didn't budge an inch. Mrs. Wilkins waited and waited for what seemed like an eternity. Finally, she said, "Leave this classroom now and go to Mr. Montgomery's office. If you don't I will have him come here to get you." Jessica stood up and dashed out of the room as quickly as possible to the probably safer environment of the principal's office.

Principal Montgomery was standing talking to his secretary, when Jessica, already in tears, stepped through the door. He ushered her into his office and gave her a tissue. When she stopped crying, he calmly asked her what happened. He knew she was in Mrs. Wilkins's class so he figured that it must have been a serious offense to provoke such a rare referral to his office. When she told him that she laughed at another student's answer and was sorry for doing so but couldn't help it, he realized that there must be more to the story but didn't press her for more details. Since it was almost lunchtime, he let her stay in his office and dismissed her to the lunchroom according to her class schedule

Mrs. Wilkins ate in her room, so Mr. Montgomery decided to stop by to hear the whole story. Before he could even ask her a question, Mrs. Wilkins said, "I want that girl to stay in your office for the rest of the day." Mr. Montgomery didn't respond immediately but sat down across from her and said,

> Sounds like a misunderstanding between the two of you. Jessica is sorry but maybe she just froze in the situation; she was caught off guard. I will have her leave lunch a little early and come and apologize to you.

Mrs. Wilkins replied, "It's not about me. She needs to apologize to Joshua and the entire class for her public act of disrespect. I need your support on this or else my class will think it is okay to disrespect another student." Mr. Montgomery replied, "It seems like this whole situation got out of hand. It doesn't have to be big deal—kids make mistakes. We all do." Mrs. Wilkins face turned red and she repeated her demand that Jessica stay out of her room for the rest of the day. Sensing that the whole situation was pretty volatile, Mr. Montgomery said, "I will keep her with me and I will call her parents. Let's talk at some point about how you could have handled this better." He turned around and walked back to his office.

He made the phone to Jessica's mother who was polite but expressed her concern that Mrs. Wilkins had mishandled the whole situation. She agreed, however, to have Jessica write notes of apology to Mrs. Wilkins and to Joshua.

After dismissal, Principal Montgomery cautiously made his way to Mrs. Wilkins's room. He reported on his phone call to Jessica's mother and how she agreed to have Jessica write two letters of apology. Mrs. Wilkins just listened and replied, "Okay" and returned to grading her papers. He decided not to discuss the problem further and returned to his office.

About an hour later, when he was sitting at his desk, he looked at the parking lot and saw three teachers standing around Mrs. Wilkins who was talking in an animated way.

Later that night when he was at home working at his desk, he received a call from the superintendent of schools. Mr. Montgomery asked if there was an emergency. The superintendent replied, "No emergency, but I am very concerned about reports I have heard about how you are not supporting teachers when it comes to discipline."

Mr. Montgomery held the phone away from his ear and stared down at his desk.

Questions

How do you think Mrs. Wilkins is regarded in this community?
What does "she has seen many principals come and go" mean to you?
What do you think of Mr. Montgomery's approach to doing his job?
Why do you think Jessica would smile when she saw other students get disciplined?
Why did Mrs. Wilkins say, "it's not about me"?
What do you think of Mr. Montgomery's handling of this problem?
What would you recommend that he might do differently?
Why did the superintendent call him at home at night?
What do you think the outcome of this situation will be?
Who made the most serious mistake?

Commentary

Many people think that schools, or education in general, should be above politics, but anyone who has worked in the field of education would say that is wishful thinking. On the surface it might appear that schools have a top/down hierarchical power structure, but the real power is often concealed until it's threatened in some way.

The situation described in this tale originated in the mistake that Joshua made in not answering correctly. Mrs. Wilkins might have been trying to catch him not paying attention (his mistake that led to his mistaken answer). Jessica's laughing nervously was a mistake that led to her being reprimanded publicly. From there the mistakes seem to increase quickly and exponentially. In fact, every person in this scenario could be viewed as having made a mistake.

This situation, however, becomes explosive when a mistake is immediately viewed as something that *shouldn't have happened* with the person who made the mistake being blamed for it. It is human nature for people to avoid absorbing blame or having their mistake be publicly condemned. When the mistake carries the implication that something is wrong about the person making it, those who have power will use it to shift the blame to someone else, while those with less power are unable to do so. This is why blame so easily travels downward towards those with little or no power.

To untangle this tale, one would have to do an instant replay of the situation. What if Mrs. Wilkins had a more tolerant attitude towards mistakes? What if she said something like, "We all day dream a bit and when we do we might not be able to answer a question correctly." Jessica might not have laughed nervously because the environment would be less tense—mistakes would no longer carry the onus of "blame".

This atmosphere of fear and blame surrounding mistakes in school tends to escalate negative emotions and exacerbate most problems. In addition, in that type of atmosphere most people invest a lot of time and energy denying that they made mistakes. Conversely, when mistakes are considered par for the course of any human enterprise, people are more able to relax and, ironically, mistakes become part of the learning process.

9

Nathan's Office

Melissa was excited to do her student teaching in second grade. She had heard that Ms. Russell's classroom was very different from other classrooms and was curious to know why.

When she walked into the classroom for the first time, it seemed like a lot of classrooms she had observed. The students sat at rectangular tables that had baskets of pencils, crayons and scissors in the center for the students to share. There was a carpeted area that was used for circle times when the students gathered in the morning. The room was filled with bookcases full of books and student artwork decorated the walls.

She did notice something that seemed out of place. In a corner of the room was an area that looked like a mini-office. It had a desk, a chair, a bookcase, wastebasket, and what looked like IN and OUT baskets on top of the bookcase. At first, she thought that this might be a timeout area or place where students could go to take a break to cool off if they were having trouble. That was not the case, because she looked at another spot in the room and it had a beanbag chair, pillows and a sign that read, "Take a break spot".

As the students rushed into the room, each one grabbed a book off the shelf and started reading. Melissa was impressed to see this as "their first thing to do" morning habit. After about ten minutes, a student walked around the room with a sign that said, "Two minutes to Circle." Sure enough, after two minutes another student walked around with a timer that gently beeped until all of the students gathered in their spots at the circle; every student did except one. That student, whose name was Nathan, headed directly over to the corner office.

Melissa sat in the circle and chatted with the students until Ms. Russell started to softly sing a welcoming song that the students quickly joined in singing. By the time they finished singing the chorus a second time, they were all looking at Ms. Russell ready to hear her start the circle lesson. Melissa's attention was drawn away by what Nathan was doing in the office.

"How come he doesn't come to the circle?" "Why aren't the other kids looking at him?" "How can he get away with not doing what the other children are expected to do?" These were some of the thoughts going through her mind as she tried to pay attention to what Ms. Russell was saying.

As the circle lesson was about to end, Mr. Welsh, the school custodian, knocked on the door. He stood on the threshold and announced, "Time for the safety check." As he said it, Nathan and a girl named Natalie stood up. They went over to him and left the classroom. Ms. Russell directed the children to their tables as they began their independent work.

Melissa casually went over to the door to glance down the hallway to see what Mr. Welsh, Nathan and Natalie were doing. She saw Nathan and Natalie holding clipboards as they went to the front doors of the school. She watched each of them pull on the door bar and then make a mark on the paper on the clipboard. As Mr. Welsh, Nathan and Natalie made their way back to the classroom, Melissa went over and sat at one of the tables as the students continued their work.

Nathan and Natalie returned to the room. Natalie went to her table and Nathan returned to his office. As the day went on, the students were all engaged in a variety of lessons where they worked independently, in small groups and as a whole class.

Nathan left his desk for some lessons and went back for others. When he was at his desk, Melissa could see him take sheets from his IN box, work on them and put them in the OUT box. He also completed some puzzles and did some coloring. Melissa still had those same questions as before swirling in her mind and could hardly wait until lunchtime to ask Ms. Russell what was going on.

After they brought the class down to the cafeteria, Ms. Russell and Melissa returned to the classroom and sat down to eat lunch together and review the morning. Ms. Russell smiled at Melissa and said, "I bet you are wondering about Nathan and his office." Melissa nodded, "You read my mind."

Ms. Russell then told Nathan's story. He had difficulty being in a group and resisted all efforts to join in most large and small group activities. The child study team had suggested various strategies to use and none of them worked. Finally, Ms. Russell interviewed Nathan and discovered that he had his own office at home where he read, drew pictures and wrote simple stories. She asked him if having an office like that in school would help and he smiled and said, "Of course." Ms. Russell worked out a schedule with him so that he knew when he could go there and when he couldn't. Nathan also said that he wanted to help the school be safe, so they arranged for him to help Mr. Welsh every day to check all the doors to make sure they were locked. The other students rotated the assignment for assisting him and Mr. Welsh.

Melissa replied, "All of that is great, but is it fair to the other kids who cooperate and follow all the expectations?" Ms. Russell smiled and said, "Did you see any children not participate in any activity of the day?" Melissa replied, "No, they all seemed happy with what they were doing."

Ms. Russell saw that Melissa still seemed perplexed so she went on,

> You see I learned a lesson from my grandmother long ago that fairness wasn't about everybody getting the same or being expected to do the same thing. Fairness was really about making sure people got what they needed to participate and contribute.

Melissa replied, "But won't they see that if you act out you will get rewarded?" Ms. Russell said,

If my class operated on rewards and consequences maybe, but I think the children know that if they had a bad day or had trouble participating that we would find a way to help them. That's what communities and families do.

As Melissa sat and tried to absorb the morning and Ms. Russell's words, she slowly realized that teaching was going to be something very different from what she had experienced or expected.

Questions
What does a classroom environment say about a teacher?
Why did the corner office stand out to Melissa?
Why was Melissa impressed by how the students entered the classroom?
Why did Nathan go to his office when he did?
When Nathan went to his office, why did Melissa look at him while the students continued to attend to Ms. Russell?
How valid are Melissa's questions?
How does the lack of rewards and consequences affect how the students perceive Nathan?
What do you think of Ms. Russell's idea of fairness?
What do you think of Ms. Russell's concept of community and family applied to the classroom?

Comments
The most competent teachers can make teaching and managing a classroom look too easy. For this reason, many teachers like to have student teachers because they feel they benefit from having a fresh set of eyes to see their classroom practices. The questions and observations of new teachers give supervising teachers a welcomed opportunity to reflect on their practice. Responding to these questions allows teachers to articulate and consequently better understand why something works or doesn't. For every practice that appears to be working effectively in a classroom there is a corresponding history of that practice not initially working so effectively. This is particularly

true when a challenging student enters a classroom. The most competent teachers learn the most from these students.

What Melissa observed was an individualized adaptation, which allowed a challenging student to function within a classroom of students who didn't need such an adaptation. The remarkable aspect of this success was the attitude that Ms. Russell conveyed to her students and Melissa: this process of finding something that worked for all students became the norm for her teaching practice.

When a teacher has an attitude of making the environment fit each individual student rather than trying to make a student fit the environment, creative solutions, such as Nathan's office, almost organically emerge. Teachers like Ms. Russell, who *learn* from their students create classroom environments that successfully adapt to a wider continuum of student behavior. Melissa's experience as a student teacher could do more than teach her skills, it could change her whole perception and understanding of teaching and learning.

10

Eleven Inches

Mr. Shaffer wished he could pinpoint exactly why Jake's long hair seemed to get under his skin. Other boys in the class had even longer hair, but it was clean and pulled back into a ponytail. Their hair didn't bother him, but Jake's did; it was greasy, stringy, shoulder length and all over the place.

Jake's clothing also didn't help his appearance. He had two tee shirts that he wore to school on alternate days: a black Grateful Dead one and a white Nirvana one. He wore a torn pair of beltless black jeans that hung low on his hips. He wore dirty (originally white) Converse sneakers with no socks—even when it snowed. Mr. Shaffer wondered if Jake slept in his clothes. Thankfully, he figured that Jake must take showers regularly because at least he didn't smell bad.

Jake was well liked by his classmates. He was a good student, too. He handed in his homework on time. Jake listened intently to his math lessons, but when Mr. Shaffer looked at him all he saw was Jake brushing his hair out of his face. Mr. Shaffer felt like halting his lecture and ordering him to get a haircut, but never did.

Mr. Shaffer searched his mind for why this bothered him so much. Maybe it was the difference in their upbringing. Mr. Shaffer's father was a naval officer so he was raised to pay close attention to his appearance. He was the only faculty member to wear a jacket and tie to school every day—even in the warm spring months. His shirts, even his tee shirts, were always ironed. His pants were creased and came to the top of his well-shined shoes. He had regular monthly haircuts from the same barber who cut it the short length he preferred. As much as his wife asked him to grow a beard or mustache, he couldn't go a day without shaving. He recognized that he probably went to the extremes of neatness and order and that his reaction to Jake was a non-rational, visceral one. Mr. Shaffer, however, was proud that his professional discipline helped him keep his feelings in check, so he treated Jake with fairness and respect.

When he found out that Jake was on the varsity basketball team, he made sure to go to all the games. Mr. Shaffer was an enthusiastic fan and loudly cheered for all the players. Jake was the type of player Mr. Shaffer admired: what he lacked in talent he made up for in hustle and intensity. Mr. Shaffer was pleased to see Jake's long hair tied up in the bun atop of his head; that kept it out of his face. Mr. Shaffer wondered why Jake didn't cut it at least for the basketball season. When he saw Jake in class the next day, he came very close to telling him that, but he bit his lip and only complimented him on a good game.

Mr. Shaffer wondered what Jake's parents were like. Their son had so much going for him: bright, personable, well liked, responsible, athletic and respectful. How could they let all of those positive attributes be cancelled out or overshadowed by Jake's appearance? What type of an impression would Jake make to colleges or to any prospective employer? Mr. Shaffer didn't have any children of his own yet, but he would make sure that his son's appearance would reflect his family's values.

Mr. Shaffer was eager for the parent–teacher conference in early December right after the first marking period. He wouldn't be direct with Jake's parents about his hair or appearance. He would look for an opening to offer them some friendly advice: Jake has so much potential, so why would they risk having him judged negatively simply because of how he looked? He would offer to facilitate a friendly chat with them and Jake. He was confident that together they could get Jake to listen to reason and see the benefits of having a neater appearance.

Fortunately, Jake's grades were excellent so his positive comments could set the stage for this sensitive but necessary conversation. He would preface his comments: he wasn't being critical of Jake (or them) but was offering some friendly advice in Jake's best interests of course. He would use Jake's basketball skills and how he put his hair in a bun a way to start the discussion.

As he closed Jake's folder of assignments, Mr. Shaffer could see how pleased Jake's parents were with his progress in math. He saw the opening and went for it, "You know I went to Jake's basketball game the other night...."

Before he could finish his sentence, Jake's mother interrupted him,

> Oh yeah, basketball! Jake said it has been a real pain in the neck for him with his hair. You know he can't wait to finally get it cut—he hates having long hair. If it were up to him, he would probably keep his head shaved. His cousin died of cancer a year ago and Jake needed to do something in her memory, so ever since he has been growing his hair 11 inches long, having it cut and donating it, so it can be made into wigs for cancer patients.

Mr. Shaffer sat there and said nothing.
Jake's mother continued,

> You know he also told us to take any money we would use to buy him clothes or anything and donate it to the cancer society. We know he looks a little sloppy but we are so proud of his generous heart—what's more important, really? Don't you think so?

Mr. Shaffer nodded. For once in his life he was glad to be interrupted.

Questions

Why did Mr. Shaffer need to find out why he was bothered by Jake's hair?

Jake was a good student. How did that affect Mr. Shaffer's feelings towards him?

What do you think Mr. Shaffer thought about Jake's parents before he met them?
Why was Mr. Shaffer proud of his professional discipline?
How did Jake's basketball playing affect Mr. Shaffer?
What do you think of his strategy for bringing up the issue with Jake's parents?
How do you think Jake's reason for having long hair would affect Mr. Shaffer in the future?
Why was Mr. Shaffer so glad to be interrupted?

Comments

As much as we know that it is wrong to judge people, we seem to do it automatically all the time. It is too easy to make an assumption and form an opinion, especially when people don't conform to what we think is right or acceptable. Mr. Shaffer was aware of the judgments he was making about Jake. He also prided himself on not letting those judgments interfere with how he treated Jake. Also to his credit, he reflected upon his own values and upbringing and how they affected his feelings toward Jake. He still had a lot more to learn.

The best teachers are the best learners. Learning requires humility: a willingness to admit one's limits and shortcomings. Jake taught Mr. Shaffer about humility and how easy it is to think that only students should change. Hopefully, Mr. Shaffer will take the lesson he learned to heart and slow down his judgments about all of his future students.

5

Administrator Tales

1

The Fifteenth Hello

Ms. Sullivan, the assistant principal, liked hanging out in the hallways. It wasn't just to supervise students; it was a great opportunity to watch adolescents in action. Even though she had been a teacher for ten years and an administrator for three, she still marveled at the tangible energy you could feel emanating from students as they talked and walked together.

Every year her own personal homework assignment was to learn every student's name. She knew all the eighth-grade students' names, half of the seventh-grade students and was making progress knowing the sixth-grade students.

She knew how good it felt to hear your name said out loud and how empty it felt when it wasn't.

In addition to being assistant principal, she had the dual title of Dean of Discipline (which she disliked). Teachers sent her the students who broke the rules. For her, however, this was the worst way to 'get to know' students. Therefore, she made a point of connecting with students who might be prone to getting in trouble before they did. She felt students learned more from the discipline, if they perceived it as help coming from an ally, rather than something inflicted on them by someone with more power.

She was always on the lookout for things she could have in common with students: a favorite sports team, a popular TV show (she watched many of them only because she knew students did), a music star, or any piece of clothing she liked. The effort to find these simple connectors always paid dividends in building relationships with students.

In her effort to connect with the sixth-grade class, she would pop into classrooms to see what was going on, trying to be more visible to the students. It was in a social studies class, that she noticed Alison. Alison wore a black sweatshirt and black jeans every day. Her long brown hair always seemed to be falling in front of her face. She never raised her hand. When she walked down the hallway, she was always by herself and seemed to be hugging the wall.

AP Sullivan made sure every day to look out for Alison so she could greet her by name. She tried to smile and make eye contact but Alison put her head down when she walked by.

One week went by and five "Hello Alisons" received the same non-reply of a head down and a quickened pace as she passed.

On the second week, she tried adding "Good to see ya', Alison, have a good one" or "Hey Alison, hang in there." She still got the same non-reply and an even quicker pace.

On the third week, she tried to back off a bit by barely smiling and saying "Good morning" or simply, "Hi".

On the Monday of the fourth week, as Alison walked by, AP Sullivan accidently dropped the little note pad she usually carried. As she reached to pick it up, she was surprised to find that Alison beat her to it. Alison handed it to her and seemed to disappear. AP Sullivan turned around and yelled "thanks" hoping Alison would hear her.

The next day, as Alison walked by, AP Sullivan said, "Thanks again Alison." Expecting to see the same non-reply, she was surprised to see a slight smile and a hand raised with a quick wave.

On Wednesday, she actually heard Alison's voice, for the first time as she replied, "Hi."

On Thursday, her "Good morning, Alison" received a "Good morning" in return.

On Friday, Ms. Sullivan decided to add, "How you doing today, Alison?" and she heard Alison say, "Okay, Ms. Sullivan."

Within a month, AP Sullivan and Alison were talking to each other about TV shows and favorite songs. Alison turned out to be quite a reader and had read some books that AP Sullivan had read. It was no surprise then that one day when AP Sullivan greeted Alison and said, "How are you doing?" Alison replied, "Not so good" and she asked if they could go somewhere to talk.

After that talk, AP Sullivan introduced Alison to the school counselor who started to meet with her on a regular basis.

A few months later, AP Sullivan overheard some teachers in the faculty room sharing their amazement on the progress that they had observed in Alison. One of the teachers asked her if she had any idea why Alison had changed so much. AP Sullivan thought for a moment and then said, "It was 15 hellos." The teacher replied, "It was that simple—just saying hello?" AP Sullivan said, "Yes, but the scary thing is, I almost gave up after 12."

Questions

What do you think about AP Sullivan liking to "hang out in the hallways"?

Why do you think she disliked the title Dean of Discipline?

How does it matter if students perceive AP Sullivan as a friend rather than an enemy?

Why did Alison not reply to AP Sullivan's greetings for so long?

Why do you think AP Sullivan backed off a bit after the third week?

What is the significance of Alison picking up the dropped notebook?

What do you think was going through Alison's mind for the time preceding her first response to AP Sullivan?

Why does the teacher question AP Sullivan's response of "simply saying hello"?

What would have happened if AP Sullivan had stopped after 12 greetings?

Comments

AP Sullivan actively strove to become trustworthy to all students. It is a given that educators care for their students and it is understandable that they might just assume that students know that to be true.

Many students do trust their teachers and administrators but there is a certain percentage of students who are distrustful and even suspicious. Many times educators will say, "trust me," when they find a student who is reluctant to talk or share.

In reality, having to say that phrase "trust me" is often perceived by students as the reason why they shouldn't. Students, who have trouble trusting, have a myriad of reasons for not doing so. Ironically, the first step in gaining trust from a student is respecting this reluctance and suspicion. With this being the case, AP Sullivan had to walk a fine line between showing she cared, her desire to be trustworthy and her respect for Alison's lack of response.

This tale, however, illustrates that most students, even the most reluctant ones, deep down on some level want and need to connect with adults. Students who ultimately rise above their desperate personal circumstances usually point to one adult who believed in them when they couldn't believe in themselves. AP Sullivan clearly conceived of her role as being on the lookout for those students who need that type of person in their life. She obviously had learned that there really are no simple hellos—each one is important and in some cases, they might be the difference between a student's success and failure.

2

The Best Teacher

Principal Jones was new to the district but soon developed an admiration for his veteran colleague, Principal Smith. He thought that he would benefit from observing whomever Principal Smith considered as his best teacher, so he made an appointment to visit Principal Smith's school.

Principal Jones asked Principal Smith if he could observe the best teacher's classroom so he could see for himself what made this teacher so excellent. Principal Smith directed him to go to Ms. Henderson in Room 402. Principal Smith stated that any visitor could walk right into that room and talk to students about what they were learning without interrupting any lesson. The students were used to visitors since it was such a model classroom. Principal Smith said that the students' description of their learning would tell him what made Ms. Henderson such an excellent teacher. Principal Smith said that he had informed the teacher to expect a visitor.

As Principal Jones eagerly approached Room 402, he could hear the hum of conversations. He lightly knocked on the opened door and walked in. He observed groups of four to five students sitting at round tables. On the tables were stacks of books about insects. Each student had a notebook and a pencil. There were several packs of sticky notes on the table. He observed students writing on them and putting them on certain pages of the books they were reading. He did not immediately see any teacher or adult in the room.

He squatted down next to a student and inquired about what she was doing. She replied that the students were doing research on insects. Each student had selected one insect to research, study and write a report about. When the unit was over parents would be invited to come into the classroom to hear the students read their research reports on their insect of choice. The students were currently continuing their research and discussing their progress or any problems they were having with their research. Principal Jones randomly selected several more students to ask them the same question and he received similar answers.

He was very impressed by everything he observed and heard. He finally noticed the teacher who was sitting at a table with a small group of students. Then he saw her get up and move to another table. When he finally made eye contact with her, she got up and walked over to him. He extended his hand as he introduced himself and explained why he was in her classroom. He said,

> Ms. Henderson, I want to thank you for the great welcome that your students offered me. I also want to congratulate you on the tremendous learning that is going on in this room. I asked Principal Smith to direct me to a classroom where I could observe an excellent teacher and that is exactly what I saw. Thank you again, Ms. Henderson.

As he said this, he noticed a confused look on her face. When he finished, she looked at him and said,

> I am sorry to disappoint you but I am not Ms. Henderson, she is out sick today. I am Ms. Johnson the substitute—this is the first time I have been in this room. Principal Smith must have been mistaken and sent you to the wrong room.

Principal Jones stood there wondering how this *mistake* could have happened. "Was it a mistake?" he thought to himself.

Questions
What do you think of Principal Jones's idea of visiting Principal Smith's school?
How could Principal Smith comment on the "tremendous learning" he observed without actually seeing any instruction?
What were the elements/conditions of the classroom environment that seemed to impress Principal Smith?
Why did Principal Smith recommend that Principal Jones ask students about what they were learning?
Would you have been as impressed as Principal Smith was if you had observed what he did? Why? Why not?
Did Principal Smith make a mistake? If not, why did Principal Smith send Principal Jones to Room 402?
What effect do you think this experience would have on
Principal Jones's assessment of his teachers when he returned to his school?

Comments
Principals must articulate their vision for what makes an effective teacher. Very often their criteria are a product of the principal's own experience as a student and teacher. As principals gain experience from years of observing teachers, their vision becomes clearer and more detailed. Recently, however, there has been a recommended shift in evaluating teachers: principals should focus less on teaching and more on learning.

This shift for many educators is difficult to grasp and implement in practice. Most educators have been taught in a system based on the assumption that student learning is dependent on the direct instruction of the teacher. This story illustrates how an effective teacher can create a classroom environment that is not entirely dependent upon direct instruction or the teacher's physical presence in the room.

This renewed focus on learning requires that educators envision a different role for a teacher, that of architect or designer of the environment that will produce a different type of learning experience for the students. School leaders, therefore, must articulate and discuss with teachers what constitutes a positive learning environment.

Principal Jones values a teacher who has embraced her role as architect/designer. He must have observed over time that Ms. Henderson had designed an environment where students could continue learning in a way that was not dependent upon her presence. (Note that the observation occurred several months into the school year.) This type of environment did not happen by chance. What Principal Jones observed was a result of the teacher's investment in helping students take ownership and responsibility not just for their own learning but also for the collective learning of the class. The conditions for learning that seemed to be in place included: student autonomy, positive and focused social interaction, a purpose for learning, and a sense of making progress over time.

3

The Superintendent's Son

At the first staff meeting of the new school year, Principal Williams announced that he had met with the new superintendent. He said that she was an experienced administrator who had entered the field of education following a successful career in the military. She was fair-minded but had high standards for professional behavior, in particular for how staff interacted with students.

Principal Williams was only in his third year as principal. He had high regard for the staff and high hopes for what the school could accomplish. He was concerned about what he viewed as lapses in the language and tone of some of the staff towards certain students who seemed to always be getting in trouble. He regretted that some staff viewed these students as troublemakers who negatively affected the learning of the majority of students, who cooperated and followed the rules.

He had tried to model how to hold students accountable for their behavior while still respecting them as individuals. He corrected students in private and never in front of their peers. He refrained from shaking his finger, using sarcasm or raising his voice in anger. In addition, he believed in establishing positive relationships with all students but especially with those who experienced difficulty in school.

After making his announcement about the new superintendent he added that the superintendent's son was going to be attending their school. He said that the superintendent did not want her son to receive special or preferential treatment. Therefore, she was not indicating to anyone, including the principal, who her son was. Her husband who had a different last name (she kept her maiden name) would be enrolling him and he would be the one to interact with staff.

Since the school typically had 30-plus new students enrolling every year, the principal told the staff not to concern themselves with trying to figure out the identity of the superintendent's son. As he finished his announcement, he paused and stated emphatically

> The superintendent feels strongly that there is never any justification or acceptable excuse for treating any person with disrespect. She asked me to inform you that if you do not know how to discipline in a respectful way, that she will provide the appropriate professional development to help you learn how.

There was silence when he finished and no hands were raised with questions.

As the school year progressed the principal noticed a positive change in the quality of interactions between staff and students. He no longer heard the negative tone of voice or observed public reprimands. He saw all staff smiling more and greeting students by name. He also heard more staff saying "please" and "thank you" when giving directions to students.

After a month, referrals to the principal's office were dramatically lower than in previous school years. In general, the overall climate of the whole school had improved, as visitors to the school would go out of their way to tell him. In addition, he received no complaints from any staff about following the directive of the superintendent. The school had indeed become a better place for everyone.

Then one day a veteran teacher knocked on the principal's open office door. She didn't wait to be welcomed but strode in and stood over him, as he pushed his chair away from his desk. She looked straight at him and said, "I am outraged and frankly shocked. I just found out that our new superintendent has NO CHILDREN! You lied to us."

Principal Williams smiled and said, "You got me. I am sorry. I guess I did sort of embellish the truth a bit."

"Don't smile—there is nothing funny about lying to your staff," the angry teacher snapped.

Principal Williams stood up and replied,

> The new superintendent did say this, "I want all the students in the district to receive the same type of education and treatment that I would want for my own children. I don't have children of my own: all the students, therefore, are my children. I expect that we give them the same respect and care that we would give to our own families." So I offered what I thought was the best and most helpful interpretation of her message. I hoped it would point us in the right direction. Don't you think it did?

The veteran teacher stood there for a few seconds without saying anything. Then she turned around and walked out of the office. The principal followed her and said in a loud enough voice so she could hear him, "Thanks for your feedback."

Questions

Why do you think the principal mentioned that the superintendent was in the military?

How do you think this fact might have affected the staff?

Why do you think that after two years as principal, not all staff followed his example?

Was the principal justified in telling a false story to the staff? Why? Why not?

What do you think the superintendent would say about the principal "embellishing the truth"?

What do you think will happen once the entire staff finds out that the superintendent did not have a son in the school?

Why do you think the veteran teacher had nothing to say in reply to the principal?

Why do you think the principal thanked the veteran teacher? What would you do next if you were the principal?

Comments

Picasso said, "Art is a lie that tells the truth." The principal in this tale might use that quotation as a justification for misleading his staff. The principal might think that just quoting the superintendent would not be enough to change his staff behavior towards students. After two years of modeling what he expected to see, not all staff members were consistently respectful towards all students. Perhaps he concluded that all that really mattered was how the students were treated; he chose the lesser of two evils. In the principal's mind the ends did justify the means.

Fear is a powerful motivator for accountability. Schools do have hierarchies and the superintendent is at the top of them. Staff members were, therefore, acting in their own self-interest by repressing their inclination to give students, who misbehave or break the rules, the harsh treatment they think these students deserve.

Their respectful behavior was motivated by their fear of getting in trouble with the "top dog." Many staff members firmly believe that discipline in order to be effective needs to be delivered in a stern way, and without the fear of the superintendent hanging over them, there was no reason for them to change their ways.

Ironically, it took the threat of getting in trouble with the superintendent to motivate them to risk changing their habits of how they interacted with the students who broke the rules. The principal in his mind was only using fear as a way to get the staff to stop using fear as way to control student behavior. He was betting that students would respond positively to more respectful behavior from staff members. He also figured that once "respect" was shown to work, that it would be almost impossible to go back to "disrespect".

The principal was nudging his staff toward the behavior he was modeling for them. Some staff members were already treating all students with respect, so he just needed to have those words and actions become the social norms for how to treat students. By using the ploy of the superintendent's son to flip a few more staff to that way of treating students, he got the critical mass for making respectful treatment the social norm for how staff treated students.

The ethical question is how much, if any, "bending of the truth" is justified even if it results in better treatment for students and a better overall school environment.

4

Fault Lines

Principal Wexler was sick and tired of hearing the same complaint from a lot of the staff: she was not tough enough with the students. "How will they learn to follow the rules if they think they can get away with it?" "All the touchy-feely stuff sounds good but how about the real world—the police don't care about how you feel when you break the law." "You don't know what *these kids need.*" To many staff members, these phrases represented indisputable truths that were the foundation of school discipline.

As principal she knew how to hold students accountable without having to inflict punishments. Her guiding question for effective discipline was: what does the student need to learn in order to not make the same mistake again? Detentions and suspensions by themselves did little good if students returned to the same circumstances without having learned better ways of solving problems.

The traditional rules-and-consequences approach to discipline, however, was so entrenched with many of her staff, that any alternative approach was viewed as being laissez-faire, unrealistic and irresponsible. Principal Wexler envisioned this difference in philosophy as being a sharp dividing line between her and a significant number of her staff: a line that seemed impossible to erase.

Sometimes she felt like shouting, "Don't you realize that this punitive approach has been tried for years and years and HASN'T worked?" but, not wanting to deepen the divide or inflame the conversation, she kept these thoughts to herself.

In her calmer moments, she acknowledged that it was difficult to give up this traditional and familiar approach (no matter how ineffective) without a guaranteed and effective alternative to replace it. For many staff, the risk would be too great; therefore, no amount of data, research, or well-argued reasoning could assuage their fear of losing control over a high school of over a 1000 adolescents.

All she wanted was a safe way to begin to talk about this issue without this *either/or* thinking stifling the discussion and deepening the divide among staff.

So when the district office mandated that the staff be trained to use a new online system for recording attendance, grades, and a variety of other information, she saw an opportunity. She knew that most of the staff was not thrilled about this, so she shared her own lack of enthusiasm for it. She announced that it was mandated from the central district office, so with this challenge they were all in the same boat.

The staff assembled with their laptops every Wednesday to take a guided step-by-step training course on the new system. This training consisted of several modules each with a quiz at the end; staff had to answer at least 80 percent correct in order to move to the next module.

At the midway point in the training, the staff had to take the module 1 quiz. They had five minutes to answer ten questions and get eight correct to move to the next module.

After staff had completed the quiz, Principal Wexler asked for those who got eight or above to raise their hands. She complimented them on doing a good job. Seeing about five people not raising their hands, she announced, "Now I want those who got less than eight to stand along the wall for five minutes." Surprisingly five teachers stood up and did what they were told. The teachers who were sitting avoided looking at them.

Principal Wexler continued,

> It doesn't feel good to be standing along the wall, but when you return to retake the quiz you will be better motivated to succeed. Of course, you won't want to stand along the wall again, especially if you would be

standing there alone. The rest of you will probably work harder to avoid having that happen.

One teacher who was sitting spoke up,

> How dare you imply we weren't motivated? We are all trying our best. Tell me how standing along the wall will teach anyone to pass the quiz. Will the right answer magically pop into our head? This makes no sense at all.

When the teacher finished his statement of protest, the staff applauded.
Principal Wexler replied,

> You are absolutely right. I was wrong to imply that anyone lacked motivation. Of course you all want to succeed. There is a tutorial built into the training. That is what will help you pass the quiz. Standing along the wall for five minutes won't do anything, but make you angry at me and probably whomever inflicted this course on you.

She continued,

> Sorry for this detour, but I wanted to offer some food for thought. This situation is not that much different from issues with behavior and discipline. Most students get in trouble because they are lacking the skills to navigate the social world. They might also be carrying burdens that negatively affect how they cope with the demands of school. These students need to be held accountable for their behavior but also need support and guidance in learning better ways of solving problems, controlling their emotions and communicating.

She almost added, "End of speech," but continued:

> You know you could make a convincing argument that academic knowledge and skills are easier to learn than

social and emotional ones. For example, once you learn that 2+2=4, that's it, you know it. How do you deal with coming to school one day and your best friend is nice to you but then the next day he says something mean or insulting? Succeeding in the social emotional world is not about "will," it's about "skill." As you discovered with this training: consequences alone don't teach.

She paused and then added, "End of speech." She let out a deep breath and soaked in the silence in the room.

It was so quiet that she could hear a pin drop. She realized that it was exactly this sound that she had wanted to hear for a long, long time.

Questions

How accurate is Principal Wexler's assessment about those comments being representative of indisputable truths about discipline?

What do you think about the question that guides Principal Wexler's decision regarding school discipline?

What do you think of her decision to keep many of her thoughts to herself? Was that a good idea?

What does "having a *safe* way to discuss the issue" mean?

What do you think about Principal Wexler creating a teachable moment for the staff?

What do you think of Principal Wexler's point about social and emotional skills being more difficult that academic ones?

Why was silence such a good thing for her to hear?

What type of conversation do you think would follow that silence?

Comments

Students who don't follow the rules and defy teachers' authority threaten the order and predictability that most educators believe are essential for classrooms to function. In addition, many students who consistently cause "trouble" develop negative reputations and feelings among teachers. Teachers strongly assert that these students need to be controlled. Any failure to do so can engender both fear and resentment among educators.

Since principals have more authority and power, teachers expect them to assert their power to restore any threat to the smooth functioning of the classroom. Principals who fail in this important task risk alienating their staff and undermining their credibility. This is the dilemma that Principal Wexler faces. She also realizes that she and her staff cannot easily discuss the topic of school discipline without triggering an emotional discussion that is often disguised as a rational one.

Principal Wexler took a big risk by using the training situation to inject a different way of thinking about a problem. Staff could view what she did as being condescending and manipulative. Perhaps Principal Wexler thought that there was a bigger risk involved in continuing to let a volatile issue divide the staff and undermine her leadership.

Many people understandably prefer to ignore differences and conflicts rather than face unpleasant and unproductive discussions that can stir emotions but leave problems unresolved. Principal Wexler knew how important it was to at least create a safe space to begin the discussion of school discipline. Hearing silence following her comparison of academic and social emotional learning signaled to her that the staff was thinking about what she had to offer. She was just looking to have a little traction, a place to start the discussion without some loud voices drowning out all others.

5

Two Questions

"What have I gotten myself into?" Principal Nelson thought, as she stood in front of a high school faculty. She was an elementary principal and felt like a fish out of water.

She was there because she couldn't say "no" to her friend and colleague, Principal Ramirez, the high school principal. Principal Nelson knew how her colleague had struggled with her staff to improve the climate of the high school. She also had to admit that she was flattered to be considered an "expert" on the topic of school climate.

Principal Ramirez told her that there were staff members who didn't see any problem with using sarcasm or chastising students in front their peers. There were faculty members who claimed that their primary responsibility was to teach their subject and it was the students' responsibility to learn it. For them school climate was a nebulous term, just another educational buzz word in favor for a brief moment.

For many students, however, the high school's climate wasn't friendly. And to certain students, the climate could be hostile at times.

She admired her friend's courage for devoting the district's professional development day to the topic "Creating a Caring Community." Was she, an elementary principal, the person best suited to talk to them about it?

Now, as she stood at the lectern under a bright light and squinting into the back rows of the auditorium, she saw faculty sitting as far away from her as possible. Many were grading papers. Others were looking at laptops or checking cell phones. Some actually were looking at her, so all was not lost.

She tried to put herself in their shoes. Who was this elementary school principal anyway telling them what to do? Why was she wasting their time with some touchy-feely stuff that didn't work with high school students? Did elementary school people have to worry about students getting diplomas? Did they have to deal with parents demanding that they get their students into top colleges? Not a chance.

Sure, her school's climate team of teachers and parents had developed a program called "The Peaceful Playground." It was a success: the behavioral referrals from recess had decreased over 80 percent in five years. The staff invested a lot of time and energy in developing a sense of community in the classroom and throughout the whole building. She was rightfully proud of what the school had accomplished.

She had a terrific presentation with videos, great photos and graphics, and not too many bullet points. Too bad, however, she didn't make sure that the faculty was sitting at tables—a detail she didn't attend to because she was new to presenting outside of her school. She had intended to get the faculty to interact in small groups, but now that was an impossibility.

Stalling to collect her thoughts, she adjusted the microphone to her height. Looking again at the back rows of the auditorium, she abruptly closed her laptop and decided to ditch her presentation. She tapped the mic and said, "Thank you for inviting me and giving me your valuable time and attention." (There was no sarcasm in her voice.)

She took a deep breath and continued, "The topic today is "Creating a Caring Community." But who am I to tell you that?" She saw faculty peek up from their papers and devices and glance at her.

She proceeded, "You are a caring community. Let's prove it. Please raise your hand if you can answer YES to this question: Do you care for every student in this school?"

Every hand went up, some more quickly than others. She scanned the group and said, "I thought so. Look around—

every hand is raised. No need to create something you already have."

She picked up her laptop and leaned a little closer into the microphone to speak, "I don't think you need me. I will let you get on with your work." She quickly turned toward the side exit, walked out of the auditorium and stood to the side of the door out of sight. She heard a flurry of hushed voices. She counted to 30, which seemed to take forever.

Then she walked back into the auditorium, and now all eyes were glued to her. Standing at the lectern again, she said, "Oh, I am sorry. I forgot to ask a second question."

She had their full attention. "Raise your hand if you can answer YES to this question." She continued, pausing for a few seconds between each word, "Does every student know that each and every one of you CARES for every student in this school?" She waited and waited—again for what seemed like forever. Not one hand was raised.

Principal Nelson continued, "I'm not surprised: most faculties are where you are, answering "yes" to the first question and "no" to the second."

She stepped from behind the lectern and took three steps up the aisle. Projecting her voice, she added, "Another thing: you can't just tell students you care because they won't take your word for it."

She took a few more steps up the aisle and continued,

> But don't ignore the good news: the care is right here—you don't have to create it. Now all you have to do is communicate the care. How tragic could it be for a student to act on the belief that no one cares, when in reality everyone does? The challenge, therefore, is to find a way to answer, "yes" to *both* those questions. You must be the ones to find it. You are halfway there. I wish you all the best on your journey. Thanks again.

She stood there for a few more seconds, letting what she said linger in the air.

She went over to her friend, Principal Ramirez, who was sitting in the fifth row. She grabbed her hand and shook it, like she was passing her a baton.

Then she turned around and walked out of the auditorium. And this time she didn't return.

Questions

Was it a good idea to invite Principal Nelson to be the presenter on the professional development day? Why? Why not?
Should Principal Nelson have accepted the invitation? Why? Why not?
Why do you think some hands went up more slowly than others in answer to the first question?
Given what she knew about the faculty, why did Principal Nelson state that "you are a caring community"?
Why did she walk out of the auditorium and count to 30?
Why did Principal Nelson pause after each word of the second question?
Why do you think she added the phrase "they won't take your word for it"?
What do you think happened after Principal Nelson left?

Comments

Professional development days are common occurrences in most districts despite their questionable effectiveness. In this story, Principal Nelson was at least someone from the district, so the district wasn't paying thousands of dollars for some outside expert to come in to enlighten staff.

The problem, as Principal Nelson realized as she stood in front of the faculty, was that she lacked credibility in the eyes of the high school staff. In most districts the different levels, elementary, middle and high school seem to be on different planets with little or nothing to offer each other, even though they all have the same task of educating students.

Principal Nelson probably had very relevant, useful ideas to offer any group of educators. Being a good educator, however, who knows the importance of having a class's attention, Principal Nelson realized the content of her presentation would have little impact on her audience. She could have proceeded as planned, done her job, helped her colleague and perhaps planted a few ideas for some faculty members already inclined to care about school climate and community, or instead take a chance and try something "out of the box".

Principal Nelson decided to follow her instincts and create a "moment". Her dramatic scene got the attention of the distracted staff. Since the hard work of improving school climate really needs to come from within each school community, Principal Nelson probably thought that the best she could do was to set the stage for her colleague to initiate a difficult conversation with her faculty. After doing that, she thought, "mission accomplished", and left the scene.

6

From Point A to Point B

Ms. Watson and Ms. Morse started their jobs as elementary school principals at the same time, and both had five years' experience in their district. They shared a belief in the importance of developing a strong sense of community in each classroom and across the school as a whole.

In both of their schools, there were staff members who shared that belief and were eager to embrace any initiative based on it. There were also staff members whose practice hadn't shown that belief, but after reflection and discussion, they became open to adapting their practice. There were a few staff members who clung to the status quo and didn't see a need to invest any time or effort in changing their practice. These principals shared very similar challenges and aspirations.

To support one another, they agreed to meet every Saturday morning for coffee at a local cafe. This was a very informal meeting with no clear agenda; it gave them a time to check in and hear how things were going in both schools.

One change initiative they discussed was the practice of daily morning meetings in each classroom. As the new school year approached, both principals agreed to take the risk of proposing that teachers hold daily morning meetings of at least ten minutes. At these meetings, all the students would sit in a circle and check in with each other and the teacher.

This was not a proposal that came out the blue: both staffs had been reading about and discussing culture and climate for a while. Both principals had pooled their professional development budgets to provide summer training and ongoing after-school workshops for staff. In addition, there were teachers in both schools who had already been having morning meetings for at least a year. Although the path to staff consensus was different in both schools, both principals had every teacher on board to try this practice for at least a year.

At their Saturday meetings, this rollout of the new initiative was the main topic of their discussion. Ms. Watson in particular needed the most time to vent about how things were going, remarking,

"You know after one week, I had some teachers complaining about how late arriving students disrupted the meetings."
Ms. Morse listened and replied, "Same in our school."
Both principals shared how this problem was addressed in their schools.

"I thought that we were okay, but then I had teachers complaining about how hard it was to keep the chatter down among the students."
Ms. Morse listened and replied, "Same in our school."
Again they shared how the problem was addressed in their schools.

"Again, I thought we were okay, but I had teachers complaining that there wasn't enough time to allow every student to say something because some students talked too long."
Ms. Morse listened and said, "Same in our school."
Again they shared how the problem was addressed in their schools.

"When we started having school delays because of bad weather, some teachers complained about the time crunch they felt because of morning meetings."
Ms. Morse listened and said, "Same in our school."
Again they shared how the problem was addressed in their schools.

Finally, just the other day at a faculty meeting, two teachers spoke up and said that they were not seeing any benefits to these meetings and they couldn't justify all the hassle involved in trying to implement them. No one spoke up against them. I am not sure why.

Ms. Morse listened and said, "Thankfully that hasn't happened in our school."

Ms. Watson sighed, "Sounds like we were on the same path but how come I'm facing this and you're not? What is the difference?"

Ms. Morse replied, "I guess I forgot to tell you what I did to frame the change to our staff. Maybe that's the difference?"

Ms. Watson still a little frustrated said, "A frame made the difference? I don't get it."

Ms. Morse continued,

Well, I think every staff member has at one point in their lives experienced some type of home renovation (or at least watched it on TV)—a time when they wanted to improve some room or aspect of their living arrangement. For added effect, I showed them before and after slides of my recent kitchen renovation. I said that adding a morning meeting to our routine was like a home renovation: our school is good, and morning meetings could make it better. I asked them to imagine a house from *before (point A) to after (point B)* and to visualize what it looked in the middle.

Ms. Watson said, "That's it?"
Ms. Morse added,

Yeah, so much of life is about expectations. Some teachers tend to be perfectionists, so without changing this default expectation anything we do short of that can be viewed as a failure. The catch phrase I used (and asked everyone to write it on an index card) is what I repeat when complaints arise: **"when you are in the middle of going from Point A to Point B, EXPECT A MESS."** I guess that did the trick.

Questions

How does the distribution of attitudes about change among staff match up with your experience?

What effect did the Saturday morning meeting have on the decision to start up morning meetings?

What do you think might have happened to the initiatives of morning meetings if the two principals didn't communicate regularly?

How important is the "framing" of an issue or problem to its ultimate success or failure?

How important was having tangible images of *before* and *after* home renovations to Ms. Morse's success?

Why do you think Ms. Morse had her staff write down the phrase, "Expect a mess" on an index card?

Comments

Schools are difficult places to change for many reasons:

- The press of everyday life—too much to do and little time to do it.
- Habits are inherently hard to change even with the best intentions to do so.
- Fear of failure plus a lack of confidence in making the change.
- The availability of reasonable objections.

Since educators tend to be rational thinkers, school leaders understandably appeal to reason, data, and research to effectively make the case for a change. There is also a tendency to focus on the content of a change initiative rather than the process of change. In reality, making a change involves a lot more emotion than many school leaders realize. People who are in the business of getting people to change, like advertisers, typically employ a different route that embraces the role of emotion in change.

As arguments against change seem difficult to surmount, school leaders can overlook the impact of how an issue is framed on the outcome of a change initiative. There were three key elements that helped Ms. Morse in facilitating change: talking about the change process, using a concrete image as an analogy and an easy-to-remember catch phrase that evokes the image. Although these elements by themselves cannot do the nitty-gritty work of change, they can keep some people involved in the process from giving up and keep those on the fence from following them.

7

Three Questions

Principal Goldman thought that if his faculty were a baseball team he would have a great blend of veterans and rookies—a formula for success. But in a middle school this distribution of experience among staff created two very different teams that played against each other. Two teams he had to manage at the same time.

He could understand the veterans' point of view: they had seen too many well-intentioned initiatives come and go. And he could understand the new teachers feeling held back by colleagues who resisted change no matter what it was. This divide was the obstacle preventing their good school from becoming better. He would trade the full implementation of any initiative/program for simply getting the staff to listen and learn from each other.

He had tried too many pep talks, too many teambuilding activities and too many TED talks to motivate the staff. His vision of community, having the blend of veterans and rookies opening their arms to the students and parents was just that, "his" vision and not "our" vision. The more he tried to share his vision, the more others resisted.

He could hear the questions they didn't voice: Who was he anyway to tell them what they should be motivated to do? Didn't they work hard enough now? Wasn't the school good enough now?

The more he thought about it, the more he had to admit that they were right; he had been misguided at best or worse, just wrong.

While going for a walk late one August evening right before the start of the school year, he recalled what his first superintendent had said to him: "People want to change, but they don't want to be changed." Suddenly he had a vision of standing in front of his staff and as he started to tell them what he thought they should do, everyone held up a sign that said: **"Help us to change but don't imply that we need to."**

Now it all seemed so simple; he decided that at the first staff meeting he would stop *telling* and start *asking*.

When the staff filed into the cafeteria on the first staff day before the students arrived, there was an index card on each chair. On the large white dry erase board was the following question: **What is one thing you do to make our school a good place to be?**

He briefly stood up in front of them and said that the purpose of the meeting was to have each person answer that question and share their answer with colleagues. He would collect the cards and compile all the answers on one sheet and have it distributed to everyone within a day.

He passed out the sheet the next day (no names were listed next to the answers). Many of the answers overlapped but there was a rich variety of words and actions described. Some were as simple as "I pick up any piece of litter I see" or "I say good morning to the school secretaries."

Other answers showed just how committed some staff were to students: "I stand at the door and greet every student by name as they walk into the classroom" or "I make it a point to invite small groups of students to have lunch with me once a week." There was nothing (no comments from him) on the sheet except their collective answers to the question. Staff members could discard the sheet or they could read it and decide to try out another's answer—it was up to them.

At the next staff meeting, the same procedure was followed but there was a second question on the board, **"What is one additional thing you would be willing to try to make our school an even better place?"** Again, the answers were printed on a sheet and distributed to all staff. Principal Goldman noticed that many of these second answers were taken from the first sheet—and that was a good thing.

At the next staff meeting, the same procedure was followed and there was a third question on the board, **"What is one thing that you would recommend that everyone do to make our school a better place?"** Again, the answers were printed on a sheet and distributed to all staff. Principal Goldman again noticed that many of these recommendations were from the first and second sheet. This time he asked for volunteers to review these recommendations and to work with him to condense it down to 4–5 recommendations that would represent the most commonly held ideas.

At the next staff meeting, members from the volunteer committee presented a menu of four recommendations to the staff. After some small group discussions followed by a large group processing, the staff reached consensus to follow these two recommendations:

1. Say "please", "thank you" and "you're welcome" when giving directions to students;

2. The five and ten rule: when ten feet away from anyone smile and nod to that person and when five feet away say "Hi" and the person's name if you know it.

That was it. It was voluntary. No money or extra time was needed.

By January, visitors to the school would come to him and comment on the wonderful atmosphere they could feel in the building. Referrals to the office for behavioral issues had decreased dramatically. He observed veterans and rookies having conversations after school.

One day after touring the school the superintendent asked Principal Goldman, "So what is your secret? What can I tell the other principals to do? What do they need?" Principal Goldman paused for a few seconds and said, "They don't need anything. Every school has everything it needs to be the school it wants to be. Just ask the right questions and listen to the answers."

Questions

Why was getting "veterans and rookies" to talk together so important to him?
How accurate is Principal Goldman's assessment of how staff viewed his motivation talks?
Why did his mentor's words come to him on a walk?
How accurate was Principal Goldman's perception that staff "want to change but don't want someone to imply they need to"?
How does the first question posed to staff affirm them?
How does the second question presuppose their positive intentions?
What type of thinking does the third question stimulate in them?
What is significant about the two recommendations that the staff adopted?
How did those recommendations lead to the changes that were observed in the school?
What did Principal Goldman mean when he said that "every school has what it needs to be the school it wants to be"?

Comments

There is some research to show that people value IKEA furniture more than furniture purchased from other stores. The reason for IKEA being valued is pretty simple: the owners had an investment in assembling the furniture and took pride in doing so. This shouldn't be an unfamiliar experience: people like the recipes they make, gardeners appreciate the produce they grow and people appreciate living in houses that they helped to construct.

Principal Goldman accidentally stumbled over this phenomenon after years of trying to get his staff to work together and grow together. He realized that the resistance he faced wasn't because his staff didn't want to grow professionally, it was because they wanted to have a voice in the change process rather than have it imposed on them.

This shouldn't be a surprise: most people react negatively to criticism or even the hint of it. People need to feel affirmed and valued for the work they do and have a say in what they need to do to improve. Once they were affirmed, the veterans and newcomers worked together to make their school a better place.

The three questions and their answers integrated the positive effects of affirmation and autonomy in harnessing the energy to improve the school. The other factor that contributed to the subsequent improvement in the school was the concrete nature of the recommendations: they were easy to remember and required no skill.

Telling staff to *change the school climate* is vague and complicated. Asking staff members to follow their own recommendations of words and actions is plain and simple.

The "data" generated from the staff's answers to the three questions represented the collective knowledge and wisdom of the staff which was all the school needed to become the place it wanted to be.

8

From the Ground Up

Dr. McKeever was the new superintendent in a middle-class suburban school district that had ten elementary schools, three middle schools and two high schools. The district had a good reputation and consistently had good results on statewide tests.

For Dr. McKeever this was a problem. How could the district improve the quality of the education it provided? She knew that students in a district like this one would often achieve despite the variations of instruction they received in the classroom. To answer this question, she had to look at the data. She studied all the different types of student outcome data available and looked at the professional development offered at each of the sites. Each school, it seemed, had quite a bit of discretion on how they used their professional development budget.

After she completed her review, it was clear to her that one middle school's results were significantly better than the other schools. She reasoned that the school must have been implementing a different approach to instruction, curriculum or school climate compared to the other schools. So her next step was to interview the principal of that school, Ms. Martinez, now in her seventh year as principal, to ascertain what was different about the school.

Dr. McKeever was a "cut to the chase" type of leader, so she wasted no time and asked Principal Martinez for her professional development plan. Upon a review she found nothing different from what the other schools were doing. She was, therefore, a little perplexed and frustrated because she couldn't readily identify the missing variable that produced this school's better results.

"So how did you do it?" she asked Principal Martinez, who smiled and said, "Do what?" "Get so much better results across the board for student outcomes?" Principal Martinez replied,

> I owe it all to my brother-in-law. You see I love to grow vegetables, especially tomatoes. I have been gardening in the same spot in my yard for years now. My brother-in-law wanted to start his own garden and asked me to get some plants for him from the same greenhouse that I used....

Dr. McKeever interrupted, "Please, get to the point."

> I am. I am an experienced gardener. I use the best fertilizers, space the plants the proper distance from each other, follow the right schedule for watering, etc. My brother-in-law basically threw his plants in the ground. At harvest time, much to my chagrin, his plants yielded more tomatoes that were bigger and better than mine ... I was perplexed but then it hit me: the difference was the soil—mine was depleted and his wasn't. It's the same with education: our initiatives and programs are dependent upon the "soil" or the conditions we create for learning and growth. So, at our first staff meeting of the year, I told them my story and brought samples from my brother-in-law's garden and mine. Everyone sampled the tomatoes and they could see and taste the difference.

Dr. McKeever perked up her attention and replied, "How do you improve the soil? What program, strategy, resource did you use?" Principal Martinez smiled and said; "I asked them about our soil. What was the *ground* beneath everything we were doing?"

Principal Martinez could see the superintendent's confusion and proceeded. "We all, especially educators, have a deep knowledge of learning, that we don't tap into. We know what is needed for learning but we think we have to go looking somewhere else for the answer."

Principal Martinez described the activity she facilitated with her staff. She put them into small groups and asked them to think about the most positive learning experience they ever had, not limited to within a school. She then asked them to reflect on what made it positive. Most of the responses were not school related. Staff shared things like: learning to cook with my grandmother, tennis lessons, art class, book discussion groups, fixing lawnmowers. Some were school related: writing for the school newspaper, putting on a play, and producing a school wide news broadcast, and so on.

After she finished recounting the activity and the staff reflections, Principal Martinez reported on the common attributes that the staff found among their positive learning experiences: trusting relationships, the value or purpose of the tasks, autonomy and choice for the learner, the teacher's communicated belief in students, and a sense that progress was being made.

Dr. McKeever seemed impressed with the list but needed more specifics on how that translated into student achievement. Principal Martinez replied,

> Well, we broke into small study groups with each group taking one of the attributes. Each group's task was to report back to the whole group with a list of 4–5 specific teacher behaviors that would promote that attribute. After we had our menus, so to speak, we reached consensus on the top two of each one and committed to trying them out. At each staff meeting, we would spend 15 minutes sharing how we were doing. Over time, we started to see results that would show up in other types of data—the ones that you looked at. That's it, really. We just fertilized our soil: enriched the ground, and created the right conditions for learning.

Dr. McKeever scratched her head and said, "I am amazed. I have never heard of such an approach. How do you keep your staff on track and committed to your plan?"

Principal smiled and said. "Come with me." They walked down to the faculty room. She stopped in the doorway and pointed at the wall. There was an enlarged photo poster of two tomatoes, one small and the other larger. Under it was the caption, "Which do we want to grow?" Principal Martinez looked at Dr. McKeever's smiling face and said, "Wouldn't you say it was a no-brainer?"

Questions

What do you think of the superintendent's notion that it is hard to raise student achievement when the test scores are good?

Why do you think the superintendent thought that professional development was related to the difference in academic achievement?

How do the superintendent and principal differ in their leadership styles?

How do you see the two of them working together in the future?

How true was the principal's assertion that educators had a deep knowledge about learning?

How do you think the activity for probing the staff's positive learning experiences would be received by your staff?

How do the attributes of positive learning experiences in the tale compare with your own experience?

Do you think the poster of the different-sized tomatoes could help to keep the staff members on track and committed to the plan? Why? Why not?

Comments

There is an understandable tendency to equate data with numbers derived from standardized measures, e.g., tests, surveys, and so on. This is preferable to relying on subjective opinions or anecdotes of individuals that usually result in little real measurable progress in any domain of education. Unfortunately, however, this shift to quantifiable data has devalued the collective knowledge of educators, the qualitative data, in matters of teaching and learning. One set of data should not cancel out the other: they can co-exist and be used to reinforce each other.

The budding relationship between the superintendent and the principal has a great potential to integrate the two different types of data, although their styles might be very different. The superintendent was wise enough to know that much of the district's achievement levels were more a result of the demographics of the student body. Her desire to find the variables that could make the good results even better could be the driving force for positive change; however, it could also be counterproductive. Many staff members often interpret a leader's drive for better results as an implicit criticism of their current efforts. Most teachers want to improve their practice, but they don't always like it when someone tells them to improve, often taking the stance of "Help me, but don't imply that I need help."

Mrs. Martinez seems to have developed an effective way to help staff improve their practice without the negative inferences associated with an administrator's prompting. She makes two empowering assumptions: first, that it is preferable to focus on learning rather than just teaching, and second, that educators know a lot about learning. She was able to embody those assumptions in an accessible analogy of the soil representing the right conditions for learning. This analogy was a portal for meaningful discussions where staff members were engaged in the process of deciding on a key set of behaviors for them to adopt and practice. They could also regularly monitor their progress (via various types of data) and make necessary adjustments along the way. When staff members are empowered, and have determined the direction and the path *they* want to take (rather than the one they are told to take), all they need to stay on track are nudges like the poster of the two tomatoes.

9

Placement

In his first few years as principal, Principal Taylor was tempted to wear a disguise whenever he was out in public during the last week of the school year. This was when parents made their case to him about the teacher their child *needed* to have in the next school year. This made it difficult for him to shop in the local supermarket, buy a cup of coffee, or do anything in the community.

Unfortunately, the district's practice was to put next year's teacher's name on the final progress report that the students brought home on the last day of the school year. Some parents, therefore, picked their child up at school so they could intercept this notification and, if necessary, march into his office to complain. One time it got so bad that a parent marched her daughter into his office and told her to explain to him how horrible the next year would be. The girl did what she was told, while sobbing into her mother's handkerchief.

Fortunately, his school had excellent and competent teachers, though their personalities as well their reputations, differed among the students and their parents. Most parents were fine with their child's placement. Some however were convinced that their child matched up perfectly with one teacher and would "suffer" with another. It didn't take long for Principal Taylor to realize it was fruitless to try to reason with or change parents' mind once a placement decision didn't meet their expectations.

He worked diligently with the shared decision-making team (which included parents) to design a fair and equitable placement process that would produce heterogeneous, well-balanced and diverse class compositions. He firmly believed it would be irresponsible to all the students to do otherwise.

This process allowed for parents to provide input in writing prior to convening the placement teams of teachers. Teachers from the current grade and the next grade met to review the data on the students, read parental input, and account for the special needs of students. They developed class lists that were checked and double-checked by a variety of support staff before Principal Taylor gave them the final approval. For the sake of transparency, a description of the placement process was printed and distributed to parents.

Now after five years, there was a general consensus among the parents to respect and accept the process, so the number of complaints and dramatic scenes on the last day of school had decreased dramatically. Still, there always remained a parent or two who became very angry about their child's placement.

One such parent was Mr. Anderson, a friendly person, with whom Principal Taylor over the years had typically made small talk about the weather and sports. His two children had been good students without significant problems or complaints to be made.

Mr. Anderson, however, had liked his oldest son's teacher so much that when he found out that his other son was placed with a different teacher, he became enraged, so angry, in fact, that Principal Taylor barely recognized him when he showed up at his office door late afternoon of the last day of school.

"You have ruined my child's life!" Mr. Anderson shouted before even he sat down. Principal Taylor didn't respond immediately, which only made Mr. Anderson even more angry.

"How can you sit there and say nothing? Don't you know what you've done? Don't you care about the life of a child?"

There was even less Principal Taylor could say at that point, but he took a deep breath and decided that saying something was better than saying nothing. He ventured with, "You're right, I might be wrong, Mr. Anderson."

This was the last thing Mr. Anderson probably expected to hear, but he quickly saw his opening and said, "If you are wrong, change the placement now."

Principal Taylor, having a little more time to think, replied,

> You certainly know your child better than anyone and I appreciate how you want what's best for him: that is your job. My job is different and I have to think of all the students and make decisions using as much information as I can.

"It is the wrong decision. Change the placement!" yelled Mr. Anderson, pounding the table.

> It is certainly your right to question my competence in making these placement decisions, so here is the phone number of the superintendent, my supervisor. I suggest that you call her and raise your concerns about my job performance with her. If she thinks I made the wrong decision, she will tell me and I will change it.

Mr. Anderson grabbed the card with the phone number from Principal Taylor and stormed out of the office.

All summer and into September, Principal Taylor never heard from the superintendent or from Mr. Anderson about his son's placement.

From the first day of school and afterward, he would observe Mr. Anderson's son laughing and talking with his classmates as he walked into school and doing the same at dismissal. In addition, Principal Taylor would peek in his classroom (with the teacher who was supposed to ruin the child's life) and saw a happy student participating in every lesson.

In mid-October on parent–teacher conference day, Principal Taylor stood by the front door greeting parents. He saw Mr. Anderson and his wife as they approached the school entrance. Mr. Anderson slowed down as he passed Principal Taylor, who smiled and said, "Hi, Mr. and Mrs. Anderson, how are you doing?" Mr. Anderson returned the smile and replied, "Very good, thank you ... Quite a ballgame last night, huh?" and continued down the hall to his child's classroom to meet with the teacher.

Questions

Why do parents care so much about the teacher their child gets?
Do you think Principal Taylor changed the placement of the parent who marched her child into his office? Why? Why not?
Why didn't Principal Taylor just honor parental requests?
What do you think of the process used to place students?
Why did Principal Taylor's response of "You're right. I might be wrong." surprise Mr. Anderson?
Why did Principal Taylor's giving the card with the Superintendent's number to Mr. Anderson end the conversation so quickly?
Do you think Mr. Anderson called the Superintendent? Why? Why not?
What does Mr. Anderson's response to Principal Taylor's greeting on conference day reveal about principal–parent relationships?

Comments

What Principal Taylor discovered in his early days as principal was probably not covered in his courses on school administration. When it comes to their children and making sure they secure what's best for them, parents can easily forget their manners. Principal Taylor quickly learned the futility of simply responding to parents with reasoned arguments or reassurances.

Principal Taylor's life would be easier if he honored parental requests or if he reversed placement decisions based solely on complaints. He also realized that placement decisions shouldn't be his alone. Investing time and energy in developing a process that involved teachers and included parental input, would be the more effective way to make sensitive and important decisions regarding class compositions and teacher assignments.

When someone is attacked, it is almost impossible not to be defensive, so consequently a heated and non-productive argument usually occurs. Probably Principal Taylor had experienced enough of those situations, so he was prepared with a different strategy. He made two wise statements: one affirming and acknowledging the positive intent of Mr. Anderson, and one admitting that he could be wrong.

Mr. Anderson had no one to fight with and was left with nothing more to say. Principal Taylor was not passing the buck but simply stating the truth of the situation. He thought the placement decision was the best one he could make and wasn't going to change it, but he gave Mr. Anderson the opportunity to speak to his supervisor. This effectively avoided an argument, ended the discussion and allowed a cooling-off period for Mr. Anderson. Although we don't know for certain, Mrs. Anderson, his friends and neighbors might have helped Mr. Anderson calm down and see the situation in a different light.

6

Parent Tales

1

No Evidence

Mrs. Webster was upset because her daughter, Alicia, was upset.

One day, Alicia, who usually loved school and came home every day with a smile, ran into the house and up to her room, threw herself on the bed, pulled a pillow over her head and cried. Mrs. Webster followed her in, sat down on the bed and rubbed her back. When the crying stopped, and before Mrs. Webster could say anything, Alicia popped up and started taking off her clothes.

"Alicia, Alicia," Mrs. Webster yelled as she rushed to her. Alicia collapsed into her arms while she was still half dressed. "Tell me what happened. Let me help you," Mrs. Webster whispered into her ear. Alicia only cried out, "Let me take a bath."

Finally, after she calmed down, Alicia hesitantly told her mother what happened. "I was sitting on the bus, in the front, and these big kids walked by." She started to cry again, but continued. "They looked at me and said that I smelled and I was ugly." Mrs. Webster could feel her anger rising up, thinking of how cruel kids can be.

"Do you know who they are?" she asked, trying to stay calm. "I don't know. I put my head down and tried not to look at them," she replied. "What did they look like? Did you tell the bus driver? Did your friends see them?" Mrs. Webster rattled off those questions but realized it was too much to expect Alicia to answer. She decided to let Alicia calm down and said, "That's okay. Let's have a snack. First, go wash your face and put on your play clothes."

Alicia nodded to her mother and Mrs. Webster left the room. Alicia, however, went over to her play area, took out a pair of scissors and started to cut her hair. She was doing so when her mother returned. "Alicia, stop, sweetie," Mrs. Webster shouted. She quickly took the scissors out of Alicia's hand saying, "Why, why? Your hair! You have beautiful hair." Alicia replied, "Maybe if I cut it I won't be ugly any more. Can I take a bath now too, so I won't smell?"

Mrs. Webster decided it made no sense to talk Alicia out of feeling that way, so instead, she hugged her and led her into the kitchen for a snack. Alicia had calmed a bit and ate more than she usually did. Mrs. Webster let her watch one of her favorite TV shows to take her mind off what happened on the bus. This would also allow her to call Mr. Matthews, the principal, to tell him what happened.

Mrs. Webster never had to call the principal before with a complaint, so she was a little nervous. She didn't want to sound like an angry parent, but she had to make sure that this didn't happen again. By now it was almost 4:00 p.m. and she wondered whether the principal might have left for the day, so she was pleased when Principal Matthews answered the phone. "Hello, Lexington Avenue School, Mr. Matthews speaking." Mrs. Webster took a deep breath and in a torrent of words recounted everything to him. Principal Matthews just listened until she stopped. "Does the bus driver know about this?" he replied. Mrs. Webster with some frustration in her voice, said, "I told you everything I know." "Did your daughter tell you who the student was or what the student looked like?" Principal Matthews asked. "I told you everything I know," she repeated, but this time there was some anger mixed in with her frustration.

Having been through many of these conversations before, Principal Matthews stopped asking questions and said, "Okay, I have enough to go on, let me investigate and I will get back to you." Mrs. Webster replied, "I guess I will just have to drive Alicia back and forth to school until you guarantee me that this will not happen again." Principal Matthews replied, "I will get back to you as soon as I can."

Principal Matthews did as he said. He interviewed the bus driver who knew nothing about the incident: he didn't hear or see anything. The driver added that he typically didn't have problems with the older kids on the bus; he had a good route compared to other years. Principal Matthews talked to Alicia who reluctantly told him what her mother had reported. He talked to Alicia's friends who said they knew Alicia was upset but they didn't hear what Alicia heard. He separately interrogated every fourth and fifth-grade student and no one knew anything about what happened. Finally, he talked to Alicia's teacher to see if Alicia was apt to make up stories to get attention. The teacher said that Alicia was a happy little girl who got along with her classmates and was a delight to teach.

Principal Matthews thought about the whole incident and concluded that kids can easily misunderstand and misinterpret what is said to them, especially on a noisy and crowded bus. He reviewed the district's anti-bullying policy and the Code of Conduct and clearly there was no evidence of any violation. He knew Mrs. Webster wouldn't like what he had to report—it was one of those phone calls he dreaded, but what else could he say or do?

> Mrs. Webster, I did a thorough investigation which I will write up in a report, but I am sorry to conclude that I found no evidence that any student said what your daughter reported. There is really nothing I can do about it. Do you think it's possible your daughter misinterpreted something she overheard that wasn't directed towards her?

Mrs. Webster felt her whole body tighten. Alicia was terrified of getting on that bus and not so eager to go to school. She took a deep breath to control her rising anger and said,

> My daughter was fine until that happened and now she is terrified of getting on that bus. All she wants to do is

take baths and wants me to take her to the beauty parlor for a haircut. This is not right. She should be able to get on that bus without being frightened.

Principal Matthews paused, primarily because he had nothing more to add, but replied,

Well, I feel bad she feels that way, but I can't accuse kids of doing something if I have no evidence. I can talk to Alicia and try to tell her she has nothing to worry about. I can have the driver tell the students to treat each other with respect.

Mrs. Webster, welling up with tears and anger shouted, "So if my house was robbed and the police couldn't catch the robber, would that mean it wasn't robbed?" And with that she hung up.

Questions
What do you think of Alicia's reaction to what happened to her on the bus?
What do you think of how Mrs. Webster handled Alicia?
Describe the interaction between Mrs. Webster and Principal Matthews in the first phone call. How typical is it of parent and administrator interactions?
What could Mrs. Webster and Principal Matthews say differently that would help them work together more productively?
What do you think of Principal Matthews' investigation?
Why did the lack of evidence seem to paralyze Principal Matthews's efforts?
How accurate is Principal Matthews' explanation for why Alicia acted the way she did?
Even if no evidence ever emerged, could Principal Matthews have done or said something that would have prevented a heated conflict with Mrs. Webster?
What do you think of Mrs. Webster's statement before she hung up?
If you were Principal Matthews, how would you respond?

Comments

There's an old saying: "The operation was a success but the patient died." This tale could be considered as an example of the truth of that saying. As opposed to how the media portrays most conflicts, especially when a parent is battling an administrator, there are no good guys and bad guys involved—and that is the tragedy of the situation. Alicia needs her mother and Mr. Matthews to be teammates, not rivals.

Mrs. Webster is a caring, concerned parent who is driven to action by a desire to protect her daughter. Parents are wired to be emotional when it comes to their child. Mrs. Webster is doing her job by making a complaint and advocating for her child. However, many educators can easily dismiss complaints because the parents' emotion distorts the facts of the situation.

Principal Matthews is a caring and concerned administrator who is responsible for the well-being of hundreds of students while they are in school. If he were to be emotional in responding to problems he would quickly burn out and be ineffective in doing his job. When approaching problems, he needs to rely on the policies and procedures of the district. This reliance ensures that he is thorough and fair when he attempts to resolve the problem. By doing so, he avoids making a rash decision driven by the emotion of the moment.

The essential challenge when the parent and the administrator are both "good guys" is: how can they complement each other and work cooperatively in meeting their common goal of helping students?

In this particular case and many others like it, although parents are calling with a complaint, what they need, first and foremost, from the administrator is a recognition and affirmation of their concern for their child. Parents need to know that an administrator cares and wants to help them, i.e. they are on the same side and are not adversaries. Instead of this response, many administrators quickly assume a criminal justice mindset of gathering evidence to determine whether a crime was committed. Only with sufficient evidence can a rule infraction (crime) be ascertained. The solution therefore to most discipline issues or rule infractions, is to determine the perpetrator and then administer consequences, usually punitive ones.

Although applying discipline in the traditional way may work for some inappropriate behaviors, it is a limited tool when it comes to many other situations. Mrs. Webster and Mr. Matthews are faced with a problem that discipline can't address: how to keep a child feeling safe in the school bus environment when the evidence doesn't produce a perpetrator.

Although further along in their communication, Mr. Matthews says, "I feel bad she (Alicia) feels that way," this statement should have been his first response before getting into the facts. Administrators often think that providing some empathy to a parent could be misinterpreted as agreeing with the parent about the facts of the complaint. In reality, this initial human response is meeting the unstated need of the parent and forms the foundation for them working together, rather than in opposition. Helping Alicia feel safe shouldn't be dependent upon obtaining the evidence needed to catch and punish the perpetrator. In that way, Mr. Matthews can follow the right procedures **and** still work with Mrs. Webster to develop a plan to help Alicia get back on the bus and enjoy school again.

2

Against the Evidence

Principal Henderson and the school psychologist, Ms. Harper, faced many challenging and complex problems in their years working together. They were an effective team supporting students who struggle with the academic and social-emotional demands of school. They used data and research to guide their decision-making. Since they often met with parents as a team, they always made sure they were on the same page when they offered interventions to parents of these students.

Tyler, a second-grade student, had needed academic support since kindergarten. He had shown some problems attending to tasks, and with some fine motor skills. In reading, he was a grade level behind his peers. The principal and school psychologist had helped many students similar to Tyler in the past. They were confident that carefully designed and monitored interventions would help Tyler make significant progress and have success in school. Since they knew that the research on grade retention showed negative outcomes, in the short-term and the long term, they felt strongly that for a student like Tyler, grade retention would not be a viable option.

Principal Henderson was effective in communicating the district's philosophy and most of the parents in school knew that grade retention was not a recommended practice of the school.

In preparation for this meeting with Tyler's parents, the principal and school psychologist agreed that it would be helpful to have parent-friendly material explaining the research on grade retention, should the issue come up. They were definitely on the same page and would speak with one voice to the parents: Tyler would be better served with intensive interventions while he stayed with his peers.

A few months earlier there had been a contentious parent–teacher conference where his parents criticized his current teacher for not doing more to help him. Since the meeting was primarily about the next school year, Tyler's teacher and all the members of the student intervention team agreed that the principal should facilitate the meeting.

As they walked into the principal's office, Tyler's parents avoided eye contact and didn't respond to attempts at small talk. Principal Henderson thanked them for coming. She acknowledged that the team was there to listen and work with them to decide on what was best for Tyler.

As soon as these opening comments were finished, Tyler's father banged his fist on the table and announced, "Tyler needs to be left back. We don't care what your policy is." His wife in a softer voice stated, "We just think that he needs a chance to catch up by repeating second grade."

Principal Henderson took a deep breath and looked at the school psychologist, who was about to pull out articles explaining the pitfalls of retention. So before Ms. Harper could say anything, the principal leaned forward and said,

> Thanks for being so up front about what you want for Tyler. I appreciate your honesty. It may be our practice not to retain students but ultimately, I believe in supporting parents and honoring what they want for their children. If you want him retained, that is what we will do.

Ms. Harper's face turned red and she looked at the principal with confusion and some anger, but bit her tongue and said nothing. Tyler's parents sat back in their chairs and looked relieved that the battle they expected was not to be.

Principal Henderson said, "Okay, now that is decided, can we take some time to review Tyler's progress: what has worked for him and where he has had problems?" The parents nodded in agreement.

They spent the next hour looking at Tyler's records. Ms. Harper described the types of reading interventions that she thought would help him. The meeting proceeded well with Tyler's parents nodding in agreement with the observations being made about him as a learner. They listened intently as the principal and school psychologist outlined the various strategies that they could offer to meet his needs and how they could be offered in any grade.

As the meeting concluded, the principal said, "Can I make a suggestion?" Tyler's parents nodded. She continued,

> Since we don't have to make a decision about next year right now, why don't you take some time to digest all that we covered today? Ms. Harper has some additional information for you to read and she can be available to answer your questions should you have any.

Tyler's parents thanked both of them, shook their hands and walked out of the office.

The next day they called Ms. Harper and asked her some additional questions about Tyler and what the school could offer next year. A few hours later they called the principal and said that they wanted Tyler to be promoted with all the additional supports and services that were described to them.

Questions

What are the benefits of the principal and school psychologist working together?

Why is being on the same page so important?

Why did Tyler's parents not respond to small talk?

Why did Tyler's father begin the meeting the way he did?

Why were the parents so convinced that retention was the "answer"?

Why did the principal refrain from sharing information on grade retention research?

Why did the principal deviate from the game plan developed for the meeting?
Would the decision to retain Tyler set a precedent that would come back to haunt the school? Why? Why not?
Why did the rest of the meeting go so well?
Why did the parents change their minds and go with the alternative approach?
If the parents hadn't changed their minds, would the school retain Tyler? Why? Why not?
Was what the principal did worth the risk of implementing an unsound educational practice?

Comments

If parents aren't emotional when it comes to their children, something is wrong. Many times educators can forget that. In fact, in many situations, educators can dismiss or criticize what parents have to offer because they are not rational and are too emotional. Educators also forget that parents can very easily feel powerless in the face of a group of professionals who appear to know more than they do. Despite a school's best efforts to put parents at ease, this perceived power differential is often very difficult to overcome.

In this situation, Tyler's parents had made up their own minds about what was best for their child and knew that "the school" did not agree with them. They felt caught between a rock and a hard place and came to the meeting prepared to fight, and to win. They gave off signs that they were prepared to fight before they said anything. Since the principal assumed leadership for the meeting, she must have sensed that she and her team were in a "no-win" position. She had to make a quick decision: stay on the same page with her team or concede to the parents' wishes.

By choosing the latter, she took a calculated risk. Since she knew that ultimately the parents and school needed to work together in the present and the future, she chose to agree with the parents for the following reasons:

- ◆ Since a decision didn't have to be set in stone, agreeing with them would buy time for further discussions.

- She trusted her team would listen to her reasoning after the meeting was over.
- Even if the parents never changed their minds, she recognized that parents had ultimate authority in deciding what they wanted for their child except in cases of abuse or neglect.
- In the long run, trust was essential to establish between the parents and the school.

The principal realized that rational arguments rarely ever succeed in changing a person's mind when emotion is involved. She knew that the parents probably wanted to trust the school and work together. The principal calculated that if she "allowed" the parents to trust her team, they all could work together to come up with a solution that could gain the support of all.

3

Slack

Mr. Walker didn't look forward to parent–teacher conference day. Most of his conferences went well, but it only took one or two going off the rails to significantly increase his stress level.

What bothered him was the nit picking over grades and homework assignments. Some parents had a sense of entitlement: schools had to guarantee that their child would succeed. Yet many times when he made suggestions to parents about what they could do, they got defensive and resorted to questioning his judgment as a teacher. Compared to dealing with even a handful of these parents, teaching a class of 24 preadolescent fifth graders was a piece of cake.

At the end of the day, he knocked on the door of his colleague, Ms. Wheeler. They had both gotten their jobs at about the same time and were great supports to one another. They weren't officially a team but their informal working relationship made their job, not easy, but easier than it would be going solo.

"How'd it go?" Mr. Walker asked. Ms. Wheeler replied, "Par for the course, I guess." Mr. Walker, holding one of his student's folders, said, "Can I show you something?" Ms. Wheeler nodded so Mr. Walker sat down next to her. He showed a student's writing assignment with his comments. As he pointed to them he shared how parents questioned almost every one of them. "It seemed I was the focus of the conference, not their child," he said shaking his head. "Did you have any parents give you a hard time or is it just me?"

Ms. Wheeler replied, "I hear what you are saying. Yeah, we don't get too many parents nowadays just deferring to our judgment on anything: it can be draining."

Mr. Walker heard what she said but he didn't see the stress on her face that he knew was on his. She was actually smiling. He couldn't understand how; they were both dealing with the same demographics of kids and parents. With some trepidation he asked, "What's your secret? How come you can smile and I feel at the end of my rope?"

Ms. Wheeler took a swig out of her water bottle and reached down to give Mr. Walker his own bottle, which he thankfully accepted. "We have never talked about this, but here is what I think might be the difference." Mr. Walker started to feel a little defensive thinking that his colleague was more skillful in communicating or possibly had better ways of making comments or grading. He interjected, "You know I am so respectful, maybe even too much, I listen. I say things like *that's a good point* or *I will take that into consideration* etc."

Ms. Wheeler nodded and added, "I don't think there's much difference between you and me. Maybe it goes back to what I "trained" myself to do. Can I tell you a story?" Mr. Walker nodded.

Ms. Wheeler told him about the first time she went to the September Open House for her oldest son, Tommy. Tommy had a very experienced first-grade teacher, who in her presentation, made her feel that Tommy was in good hands. Although Open House wasn't a time for a parent conference, most parents lined up to just to say "hi" and introduce themselves. Being a teacher herself, she was aware of not taking up too much of the teacher's time.

She went on,

> I nervously approached Tommy's teacher and said, "Hi, I am Michelle Wheeler, Tommy's mom, how's it going with him?" The teacher replied, "Oh, he is a typical first grader. Like most of the other boys, he has a lot of energy, but he'll have a good year." I thanked her and let another parent have her turn.

Riding home that night, I told my husband that I liked Tommy's teacher but that somehow I felt deflated, like my balloon had been popped. I searched my mind to see if there was anything his teacher said that made me feel that way. My husband told me I was being too sensitive, but since I was a teacher, I felt I had to figure this out.

Mr. Walker listening intently said, "I probably would have agreed with your husband."

Ms. Wheeler continued,

Lying in bed, it finally hit me: it was *what she didn't say* that mattered. I needed Tommy's teacher to tell me she liked him and to let me know that she "knew" who he was—no matter how silly it might be. Tell me that he has a nice smile, or that he loves Curious George books. I needed something from her to let me know he wasn't just another boy like all the boys she taught over the years.

After that insight, I made it my assignment to find something unique about each student in my class, something that I appreciated. I wanted the first words out of my mouth to announce to parents that I liked and knew their child. It sounds simple or even stupid, but I made it a point to actually say the words, "I like ____" followed by what I appreciated. I also found that it never hurts to repeat those phrases whenever I met with parents.

Mr. Walker shook his head in disbelief, "That's it. 'I like your son or daughter'. I like my students. I figured parents would know that—you mean I need to say it?"

Ms. Wheeler replied, "Maybe coming out and saying it removes any trace of doubt in their mind. It's what I needed; maybe all parents do. It gives me some slack with them. And a little slack can go a long way."

Questions

How typical are Mr. Walker's feelings about the parents of his students?

Why might parents question a teacher's comments on a writing assignment?

Why did Mr. Walker have some trepidation in asking why Ms. Wheeler seemed less stressed?

Assuming Mr. Walker was also a parent, why wasn't he able to have more empathy for the parents of his students?

What does the statement "since I was a teacher, I felt I had to figure this out" tell you about Ms. Wheeler?

Why did Ms. Wheeler think that saying "I like your child" might sound simple or stupid?

Do you think parents really gave her more slack? Why? Why not?

How would slack manifest itself in a parent–teacher conference?

Comments

Professional amnesia is a commonplace occurrence. Teachers forget what it is like to be a student. Administrators and teachers forget what it's like to be a parent. Principals forget what it's like to be a teacher. Policymakers forget what it's like to live and work in schools. This is an understandable phenomenon since each professional role and its responsibilities can consume all of one's time and energy.

There might have been a time when parents and students deferred to a teacher and principal's authority with no questions asked. Many educators might long for those times. In retrospect, that type of unquestioning respect for those in authority often leads to people abusing that power in a variety of negative and sometimes harmful ways. Respect among people should be mutual regardless of status. Teachers and parents should respect each other and that should include asking questions or communicating concerns.

Ms. Wheeler seems to have discovered the "secret" formula for creating a mutually respectful relationship between teacher and parent. She was able to tap into her parent experience and apply it to her teacher experience. Her empathy and understanding of the needs of parents allowed her to give the affirmation that she was looking for when she was a parent. A little empathy and affirmation can go a long way to lubricating the communication between parents and teacher, especially when there might be sensitive issues to discuss. Perhaps these simple affirmative statements go unsaid because teachers forget how important it is for parents to know that the teacher likes and appreciates their child.

4

TEA Time

Mrs. Hayes's daughter, Jennifer, was a straight A student since first grade. No matter the subject, Jennifer put in the time and effort to get the highest grade she could. Now in her junior year, she was well on her way to a grade point average that would ensure that she got into the best colleges. Mrs. Hayes never had a reason to complain about a teacher, but now she faced a situation where that might have to change.

Mr. Bennett was a social studies teacher with a reputation for being different or some might say eccentric. He wore a tie every day (some days it was a bow tie). He ate lunch in the cafeteria with the students; he stood in the hallway during transitions and greeted each student by name as they filed into the classroom. So Mrs. Hayes knew his reputation from her friends and told her daughter to be prepared for a teacher who was "different". She liked what she heard about him, but she wasn't prepared for what Jennifer reported about the first week of school.

Jennifer said that on the first day of class, when the students walked into the classroom, all the desks were pushed against the wall. Mr. Bennett stood in the middle of the room, saying nothing, as he observed the students react to this situation. Jennifer said that everyone was confused. What should they do: grab a chair, sit on the floor, keep standing, talk or be silent? Mrs. Hayes thought that this was unusual but nothing that should warrant a complaint. She told Jennifer to focus on the positive. She should get used to eccentric teachers now, because she would probably have them in college.

The next day, Jessica said that Mr. Bennett explained his reason for how he started the school year. He taught American History so he wanted the students to work together and make decisions like the Founding Fathers did. The students should decide on the best way to arrange the classroom and on their classroom rules.

Jennifer also conveyed one statement that confused her. Mr. Bennett announced that students didn't have to do what he said, if it made no sense to them. He wanted them to question authority. Jennifer initially thought that this would create chaos until he explained that it was his job to provide the *MVP* to them: the *meaning, value and purpose* of everything they did. If they didn't see the point of what they were learning, then they should question it. He would try to answer and then the class could discuss it.

Mrs. Hayes listened to these unusual classroom practices and felt that they provided Jennifer with much food for thought. Mr. Bennett's grading practices, however, were too disturbing to ignore. He announced that when it came to unit tests, students should let him know when they felt they prepared to get at least 85 percent correct and then he would administer the test to them. For Mrs. Hayes this was too much to take; it wasn't fair to hard working, always prepared, students like Jennifer. Besides what value would Jennifer's A be, if everyone in the class got B+ or above.

So Mrs. Hayes made the phone call that she had never made before. With some trepidation she said, "Mr. Bennett, I have a serious concern about your test taking policy and how it affects my daughter, Jennifer." He replied,

> Well Mrs. Hayes, first of all, I want to thank you for calling. I need parent feedback especially about their child; it will only help me do my job better. I know it's not easy to call a teacher with an issue.

Mrs. Hayes felt relieved.

They agreed to meet at 4:00 p.m. in his classroom. When Mrs. Hayes walked in, she was surprised to see a pot of tea on the table with two cups next to it along with a bowl of sugar and pitcher of milk. Mr. Bennett joked, "I didn't know if you wanted tea or not, but I think 4 o'clock is tea time in a lot of places." Mrs. Hayes just replied, "Sure. Thank you."

Mrs. Hayes explained her concerns and Mr. Bennett listened carefully as he sipped his tea. When she finished, he thanked her again and explained why he had such a policy.

> You see this class is about American History. I don't want the students to just learn dates and facts; I want them to experience and know in their hearts and minds what our country is about and what it means to be a citizen. This class might be the last opportunity for that, so it's my professional and civic responsibility to make sure that every student masters and fully comprehends the content of this course.

Mrs. Hayes listened, and asked some questions, but realized that Mr. Bennett's *MVP* was hard to dispute. Besides Jennifer would still get her A, no matter the policy. Yet she still had to ask, "How did you come up with this policy? It is so different from the other teachers."

Mr. Bennett smiled and replied,

> I never understood how learning became a competitive sport in school. Did it take you longer to ride a bike than your friend? We take our driver's test when we are ready to pass it; everybody needs to know how to drive the right way for our roads to be safe. I don't think it should be any different for citizenship.

Mrs. Hayes listened closely, and in her heart, she knew he was right.

They made small talk, finishing their tea. As she was about to leave, Mrs. Hayes, asked, "Why did we have tea? It was nice, but not necessary." Mr. Bennett smiled and said,

Well, it's necessary for me. I try to do three things in every meeting with parents: **T**hank them, **E**mpathize and **A**cknowledge what we are trying to do together for their child. **TEA** is the best formula for a conversation and I need a concrete reminder.

And with that he picked up his teacup and took his last sip.

Questions

How did Mrs. Hayes view her daughter's education?
Why would Mr. Bennett be viewed as eccentric?
Why do you think Jennifer reported what happened in class to her mother?
Why was Mrs. Hayes surprised to hear Mr. Bennett respond to her phone call the way he did?
What do you think Mr. Bennett meant when he said it might be the students' last opportunity to learn how to be a citizen?
Why do you think Mr. Bennett uses acronyms like MVP and TEA time?

Comments

Compared to the experience of many parents, Mrs. Hayes has had smooth sailing with her daughter's education. Mrs. Hayes and her daughter had a clear goal in mind that was well within reach. Good grades were the ticket to a topnotch college and a successful life. No wonder Jennifer would report to her mother anything that might deviate in the slightest from the typical school experience and its concomitant success.

    Mrs. Hayes was an open-minded person and knew that her daughter could possibly benefit from a teacher who was different. Many traditional classroom practices could be changed with no detrimental effects for students like Jennifer. Grades, however, were a different matter. They were so essential for future success that any slight change in grading practice would set off alarms for Jennifer and her mother.

    When Mrs. Hayes called with a complaint she was probably expecting a degree of defensiveness from Mr. Bennett. She was prepared to counter his explanations with more convincing ones representing her daughter's needs. Once she heard the words "thank you" her whole anticipatory set for her exchange with him radically changed.

Mr. Bennett was probably used to explaining his practices to parents, so he knew the importance of listening rather than automatically falling into the position of defending his views. He also had confidence that a positive and open atmosphere for a discussion would make it easier for parents to listen to what he had to offer.

He needed to listen before he could expect a parent to listen to him. He knew that listening, especially if one's views and practices were being questioned and challenged, was difficult to do. His *tea time* helped him listen and create a civil and respectful conversation with parents.

5

At the Round Table

Ms. Polanco, the school principal, thought Tara and Jessica were mirror images of each other. Each was an outstanding student, well-liked by peers, and excelled in music and sports. They also lived on the same block, and maybe that was the problem.

Tara had a circle of girlfriends. They looked up to her and wanted her approval. Jessica had a different circle and likewise they also looked up to her and wanted her approval. Somehow Tara and Jessica and their circles slowly and imperceptibly turned into rivals.

Since these circles of friends encompassed almost every girl in fifth grade, everything Tara and Jessica did or said was scrutinized and became fodder for whispered conversations and rumors. This situation was exacerbated by the fact that each girl strove for perfection and, therefore, became hurt when their slightest mistake or misstep was spread throughout fifth grade by their rival's circle of friends.

For example, if Tara didn't answer a question correctly in class, Jessica's circle made sure that everyone knew this. If Jessica happened to wear something that Tara's circle didn't like, everyone knew about it. These circles of friends created a vicious cycle of put downs, snide comments, passed notes, facial gestures and hushed whispers.

Rumors about each girl spread throughout fifth grade. No one could tell who started a rumor or knew when it started. The whole situation seemed like it would never end, and would only get worse the longer it continued. All the girls involved seemed unable to extricate themselves from this unwittingly created predicament.

Tara and Jessica would go home at the end of the school day and report to their parents on the "horrible" things that were being said about them. Although Tara and Jessica's parents lived in the same neighborhood, they were not friendly with each other; they had their own conflicts over the years. So when each girl returned home and reported what the other girl had done to her, neither set of parents were surprised. They also became increasingly angry after each new incident.

Feeling helpless about what was happening to their daughters, each set of parents decided to complain to Principal Polanco. She would listen politely to their complaints and take notes as they told what had happened to their daughters. Of course, Tara's parents said Jessica was the one who caused the trouble and vice versa with Jessica's parents.

When Principal Polanco began to share with each set of parents what the other set had said, both sets of parents vehemently declared that the other was not to be believed. After a week of these phone calls, it seemed like the parents had a competition to see who could issue the first complaint about the latest "atrocity" that their child had suffered. Typically, Principal Polanco would be on the phone with one set of parents while the other line was lighting up with the other parent's incoming call.

After two weeks of dueling phone calls with the insistent expectation that she discipline the other child, Principal Polanco knew two things: neither girl was entirely to blame and this situation had to stop. She also realized that if the parents remained in conflict, just speaking to the girls would do little good.

She decided that the best approach would be to have both sets of parents meet with her and the social worker, Ms. Wood. She knew that the parents would be reluctant to be in the same room with each other. She also knew that having them together could make the situation worse. She searched in her mind for some common ground to find for the parents, so that they could come to the meeting with a more positive mindset.

On her ride home one day after another round of dueling phone calls, she recalled each parent stating one thing emphatically, "This has to stop ... it's getting out of hand." Of course, their version of stopping it meant for the principal to pick their side and discipline the other girl, but nonetheless, they did have one thing in common: they were both tired and needed it to stop.

After consulting with Ms. Wood, they worked on figuring out the best way to structure the meeting so they could reach their common goal of resolving this problem.

They realized that they needed some ground rules for the meeting before it began. They agreed on two essential ones:

- No issues from the past could be brought up—the focus of the meeting would be on solutions from that point forward.
- No disparaging comments could be made about anyone.

Both sets of parents initially balked at the idea of a meeting, but they reluctantly agreed when Principal Polanco reminded them that the problems would increase exponentially once the girls entered middle school. She emphasized that it was in both of their interests to act now rather than later. The parents also agreed on the ground rules for the meeting.

They would meet in the principal's office after school, and have their girls wait outside in separate locations. If the parents reached agreement on a plan to move forward, then the girls would be invited into the office to sit at the round table with their parents, the principal and social worker.

Both sets of parents entered the room with their heads down, doing their best to avoid eye contact with the other parents. Principal Polanco thanked them for coming and acknowledged that it was a difficult situation for everyone. She thanked them for agreeing to the ground rules, and expressed confidence that they would all do what was best for their children. She followed those statements with praise for the great job they did raising such wonderful girls who were full of so much potential.

From that point on, both sets of parents appeared more relaxed and readily agreed to tell their girls that they were all caught in a vicious cycle and that no one was to blame. All four parents agreed to state that both girls were good students and great kids. They would also state that they needed to respect each other from that point on. They also agreed to tell the girls to convey that same message to their friends: the rumors and criticisms needed to stop.

The girls entered the room nervously but appeared surprised to see their parents sitting at the same round table with the principal and social worker. Principal Polanco made opening remarks similar to the ones she said to their parents, but it was the parents who took turns repeating their expectations for what the girls needed to do in the future. The girls, just like their parents, looked more relaxed and relieved, like a weight had been lifted from their shoulders. At the end of the meeting, everyone shook hands with each other and the conversation shifted to typical small talk about the weather and upcoming school events.

A week went by and Principal Polanco called each set of parents. Their reports were the same: their girls seemed to be rekindling their friendship from second grade and consequently all was well.

When Principal Polanco reported the positive news to the social worker, Wood complimented her on how well she had handled the meeting. Principal Polanco smiled and replied, "Everything we said was important but I think what really did the trick was having the girls see everyone sitting at the round table—that told them we were on the same team rooting for them."

Ms. Wood replied, "Yeah, you know I bet both girls were just waiting for their parents to give them permission to be friends again."

Questions

Why do some girls have a circle of friends around them?
How aware do you think the teachers were of this rivalry between the circles of friends?

How did the girls' need for perfection contribute to the problem of the rivalry?
Was this a bullying situation? Explain.
Why do you think the principal concluded that just speaking to the girls would not resolve the problem?
Why was it important to find something that all the participants had in common as the basis for having the meeting?
Why are ground rules important for meetings?
How did Ms. Polanco's opening comments affect how the meeting proceeded?
Why do you think Ms. Polanco thought that the round table was so important?
What did Ms. Wood mean when she said that the girls were waiting for their parents to give them permission to be friendly?

Comments

This situation was complex to say the least: there was no predetermined solution that could easily be applied to resolve the problem. It was a challenge to all involved because the tendency to blame others narrows how people view problems and impedes their ability to find solutions. This was a problem where the principal and social worker had to *learn on the go:* it was teaching them as they wrestled with it.

Principal Polanco's strength was her patience and ability to help the parents gain some perspective and understanding of the problem. Instead of looking for quick fixes, she employed a variety of skills that she had learned over many years of working with people:

- ◆ Reframed the situation as an opportunity for the parents to resolve a problem before the girls went to middle school. This allowed the meeting to be viewed in a positive light and unite the parents in their common goal of wanting what was best for their children.
- ◆ Focused on the future and solutions rather than the past. She realized that it would be impossible to sort out "who did what and when to whom." By getting the parents to

agree to leave the past out of the discussion, the issue of "whom to blame" was taken off the table.
- ♦ Relied on getting the process right and trusting that it would find the right solution. If people can productively discuss problems in a safe atmosphere, their combined "wisdom" usually discovers a solution that will work.
- ♦ Affirmed the parents and the girls at the onset of the meeting. A simple statement of the obvious, that the parents should be proud of their daughters, too often goes unsaid.
- ♦ Helped parents to see the big picture and put this momentary problem in its proper context: more of a bump in the road rather than a disaster.

Ms. Wood's insight that the parents gave their children permission to be friends again recognized the tendency for children to sense what their parents want from them even if that expectation is never overtly stated. In a way, the girls were serving as proxies for their parents. When they all were sitting at the round table, the girls could tangibly sense that peace had been restored and the way had been cleared for them to re-discover what they had in common and their lost friendship.

6

Celebrating the Holidays

Mrs. Lindsey loved everything about her son's new elementary school until she went to the winter concert. The problem was, that unlike her previous elementary school, it was a winter concert, not a holiday one. To make matters worse, it was in January not December.

Her son's previous school had a Christmas tree in the lobby and the principal, even though he was Jewish, wore a Santa hat on the day before the holiday break. He would greet visitors with "Merry Christmas" and even add a "ho, ho, ho" for good measure. When she went to her new school, staff greeted her with "Happy Holidays" and she always replied, "Merry Christmas". Although this was not a big deal to her, she had to admit that on some level it did bother her.

Mrs. Lindsey had just about made up her mind to let this go, until Principal Berger called her up one day. She was a very cordial, friendly principal. Her practice was to phone parents who were new to the school and ask how things were going. Mrs. Lindsey initially shared the positive things about the school: great teachers, warm atmosphere, great enrichment activities, and high level of parent involvement. Then she took a deep breath and spoke from her heart,

> I don't like to be negative but I find it a little odd that the school seems to be ignoring Christmas time. I know that it can be overkill on TV but Christmas is prominent in

most kids' lives. How can it be overlooked in school? What message does that send to the kids?

After a few seconds of silence, Principal Berger replied,

Well, thank you for your honesty. I appreciate how you feel, but our school being near a university has a pretty diverse population of families from different countries, so we don't want to honor one religion or tradition over other ones.

Mrs. Lindsey said, "This school is more diverse, but is pretending that holidays or traditions don't exist the best response?" Principal Berger replied, "I hadn't thought about it that way. We have a shared leadership team at our school—would you be willing to attend our next meeting and share your thoughts?"

Mrs. Lindsey said "yes", thinking that one meeting would suffice to make her point. Surely, she thought, it wouldn't be unreasonable to add some non-religious Christmas songs to the concert along with some Hanukkah ones. At the first meeting, the seven teachers and the three parents on the leadership team expressed very different opinions: some wanted Christmas re-established, some wanted the status quo, others wanted a multicultural approach and some were afraid of violating the separation of church and state.

After over an hour of this discussion, all the participants realized that there were more questions than answers and more problems than solutions. After two very similar team meetings, Principal Berger suggested that a task force be established to focus on the issue of holidays in the school. Mrs. Lindsey agreed to co-chair it with the principal.

When Principal Berger and Mrs. Lindsey met to prepare for the first task force meeting, they agreed that they needed more parents to join them as well as the input from the local priest, minister, rabbi and representatives from a Hindu temple and Islamic mosque. Principal Berger invited the district's lawyer to guide them regarding the legal aspects of what they were doing.

As a result of all this time and energy, the issue of celebrating the holiday gained more attention and generated more controversy than it ever had before. At one point a member of the task force exclaimed to no one in particular, "How did we get involved with this in the first place? Couldn't we have left well enough alone?" No one answered and Mrs. Lindsey prayed that Principal Berger wouldn't look at her.

The task force looked for policies to tell them what they could do or not do, but they found none that were that definitive. What they found was: bottom line, as long as they didn't overtly promote or endorse one religion over other ones, the school community could determine for itself, based on their own needs, how they wanted to recognize and celebrate holidays or not to do so at all.

After one year, the task force drafted a set of guidelines for how holidays could be addressed in the school. The next year, the task force collected questions from parents and drafted a question and answer document where they articulated what they learned; this was distributed to all members of the school community. In addition, a group of parents volunteered to work with students to decorate a bulletin board on a monthly basis highlighting various cultural holidays. The task force recommended having the winter concert moved to December where it could feature a variety of seasonable songs, including non-religious Christmas songs.

After three years, Mrs. Lindsey's youngest child was now in third grade and her oldest son had moved on to middle school. The task force had disbanded and the issue of celebrating holidays became a non-issue.

One day Mrs. Lindsey stopped by Principal Berger's office—they were very at ease with one another. In the course of their conversation she said,

> I regretted mentioning this issue to you at times, especially when we got bogged down in problems and questions. I hope the can of worms that I opened up wasn't too much of a pain in the neck for you.

Principal Berger replied,

> Yeah, I thought this problem would never go away. I looked at my colleagues' schools and wondered why they weren't going through what we were. But as a result of what we did, I feel that our school community has the confidence to handle any problem or issue that might arise. We started out thinking that we were going to solve a problem but the problem ended up solving us—changing us for the better. Thank you.

Questions

How did being Jewish allow the previous principal to be more demonstrative concerning Christmas?
How did Principal Berger's phone call affect Mrs. Lindsay?
What would have happened if the phone call hadn't been made?
How would you characterize the work that the task force did?
How did the school benefit from its holiday problem?
How did the issue become a non-issue?
What did Principal Berger mean when she said that the "problem ended up solving us"?

Comments

Problems have a bad reputation in our culture. Advertisers know this. We are bombarded with ads for products that promise ease, convenience, and hassle-free experiences. When we find ourselves in the midst of a problem, our first reaction is to want it to go away. Schools are not immune from these feelings about problems. Educators want classrooms to function smoothly, schedules to be on time, students to cooperate, and parents to be happy.

The great irony is this: we learn very little from a problem-free experience or when life is going as we think it should. We learn from our mistakes, our failures and our problems, all of which are inevitable and are integral to our lives. Since schools are supposed to be places of learning, problems should be welcomed and embraced as great opportunities.

Principal Berger seemed to have intuitively known this. She must have known that checking in with parents who are new to her school could be interpreted as a way of inviting trouble. She must have known that every school culture has trouble seeing itself; therefore, seeking feedback from parents new to the school was vital to the process of continuous growth and improvement. In addition, a true partnership with parents means more than asking them to coordinate fundraisers or automatically supporting school initiatives.

Schools become healthier and more effective, when parents and educators develop open and honest relationships that enable them to freely discuss a range of issues and problems. This type of relationship ensures that the school community learns together in the process of addressing problems. This type of partnership, plus using the right type of process, usually produces creative solutions, which never would have happened without the interplay of differing perspectives and voices.

7

Shame

At 4:30 p.m. Mr. Woodward, a middle school principal, usually expected a phone call from a parent with some complaint or issue, so when he heard Assistant Principal Williams' voice from his son's high school, his heart skipped a beat. His son, Richard, had a history of troubles in school, academically and behaviorally, so he wasn't surprised.

He hesitantly asked, "What now?"

AP Williams first reassured him that no one was hurt but that Richard had done something that needed immediate attention.

"Could you and your wife meet me in my office within the hour? Richard is here. It would be best to find out what happened in person."

Mr. Woodward called his wife and swung by their house to pick her up. They got into a typical argument over who was the most responsible for Richard's problems, but they grew quiet as they pulled into the parking lot.

Before getting out of the car, Mr. Woodward turned to his wife and said, "Do you know how embarrassing this is for me being a principal? Every day I hear our staff blame parents for what their kids do. What does the high school staff think about us?"

When they walked into AP Ms. Williams' office, Richard was next to Principal Price; he sat motionless staring at the floor. Since AP Williams was also the Dean of Discipline, she welcomed them and initiated the meeting. Mrs. Woodward sat next to Richard and put a hand on his shoulder. Mr. Woodward sat down but didn't look at his son.

AP Williams handed them a sheet of paper filled with printed emails and text messages all concerning Richard's language arts teacher, Mr. Jacobs. Some were just derogatory comments about his appearance but other comments accused him of sexual harassment towards certain unnamed students. Mrs. Woodward just shook her head in disbelief. Mr. Woodward almost crumbled up the paper. Richard kept looking down at the floor.

AP Williams spoke next,

> Fortunately another student was aware of these and brought them to my attention; they originated with Richard. However, to Richard's credit when I confronted him with these comments he said he made them up; they were false. He also accepted responsibility for spreading them.

Mr. Woodward glanced over at his son but said nothing.

AP Williams looked at Richard and said, "Would you tell your parents why you did this?"

Richard looking only at AP Williams replied, "I wanted to get even with him. He puts kids down in class with sarcastic comments. All the kids hate him. I guess I wanted him to get fired—I was stupid."

AP Williams continued,

> These could be considered criminal offenses, but fortunately for Richard, Mr. Jacobs is not going to file criminal charges. He is content to let the school discipline him. Richard has already apologized in person and in writing to him. We will however be transferring him out of his language arts class after he serves his suspension.

Mr. Woodward and his wife sat silently as they proceeded with the technical details of suspending a student. Details Mr.

Woodward knew too well. He thanked AP Williams and Principal Price for how well they handled the whole situation, but before he stood up to leave, he looked at his son and raised his voice, "I am so ashamed of you. You know better. How could you be so stupid and irresponsible? You screw up all the time. I am sick and tired of this. Get your act together or else, you hear me?"

As Mr. Woodard said this, Mrs. Woodward reached over and squeezed his arm trying to get him to stop before too much damage was done. Richard continued to look down at the floor but his face had turned red. When Mr. Woodward finished his tirade, they all sat in silent for what seemed an eternity.

Then they all stood up and shook hands. Mrs. Woodward went over to Richard and put her arm around him and they walked out of the office. Principal Price, who knew Mr. Woodward professionally, asked if he could talk to him for a minute. Mr. Woodward nodded.

Principal Price took a deep breath and proceeded to tell Mr. Woodward the story of his son, Joseph. Joseph had "screwed up" a lot worse than Richard. He had worked through a lot of issues. He was now married with kids and had a good job.

Principal Price added,

> I felt a lot like you and was ashamed for my failure as a father. I could only see a pretty bleak future for him. Joseph's therapist, however, told me point blank that he was a good kid. He said that Joseph needed me to believe in him despite what he did. To tell you the truth that comment stopped me in my tracks. The therapist was right and I was wrong.

Mr. Woodward felt tears welling up but fought them back. He whispered, "Thanks for sharing that." Principal Price found a piece of paper and wrote down the name of Joseph's therapist and the words "Habitat for Humanity". Principal Price continued,

> You know, Joseph got trapped inside an identity in school that he couldn't shake off. He needed to find a

different, positive identity outside of school. He went on a week-long Habitat for Humanity building project with his church youth group. It made a big difference for him.

Mr. Woodward shook Principal Price's hand again saying, "Thank you so much."

Outside the office, Mr. Woodward looked at his wife who still had her arm around Richard. He stood in front of them and said, "I'm sorry I lost it in there. I didn't mean what I said. It was just my anger talking. We are going to get through this. It will all turn out okay." Then he put his arm around Richard and the three of them walked to the car together.

Questions

Why did Mr. Woodward's heart skip a beat when he heard the assistant principal's voice?

How did being an administrator make him more embarrassed than another parent might be?

What do you think of the reasons Richard gave for why he did what he did?

Why did Mr. and Mrs. Woodward act differently toward Richard?

Why did Principal Price share his story with Mr. Woodward?

What do you think of Principal Price's explanation of his son needing a different identity?

What would have happened to the Woodward family if Principal Price hadn't shared his story?

Comments

Mr. Woodward, a school administrator, found it very difficult to be on the receiving end of "bad news" from school. He was much more comfortable making the call to parents. As much as adults should know that children and adolescents are "works in progress", the expectation that their own children should be successful in school at all times can become a significant burden for parents. This expectation is especially strong for professional educators, since they feel that they *should* be more effective than other parents at raising children. Their children shouldn't be the ones who get in trouble.

Mr. Woodward, knowing that the teachers in his school often attributed the behavioral problems that students have to their parents, knew there was a pretty good chance that staff at the high school would be judgmental about his parenting. This sense of shame and embarrassment made it difficult for him to see beyond his anger towards his son. Not only did his son do something mean and stupid, he made his family look bad. This sense of shame and anger had the great potential for making the situation even worse for Richard and the entire family.

This is why the empathy of Principal Price was so critical in turning the whole situation around for the Woodward family. Principal Price did not have to tell the story of his son, but he must have been in the same emotional space as Mr. Woodward. He knew that for Richard to turn around his behavior at school, his family had to believe in him and offer him support and guidance. Fortunately, Principal Price was not afraid of having his empathy be misconstrued as being soft or wishy-washy. Principal Price's empathy toward Richard and his family opened the door for Mr. Woodward to get past his anger and offer the support his son needed in creating a more positive identity.